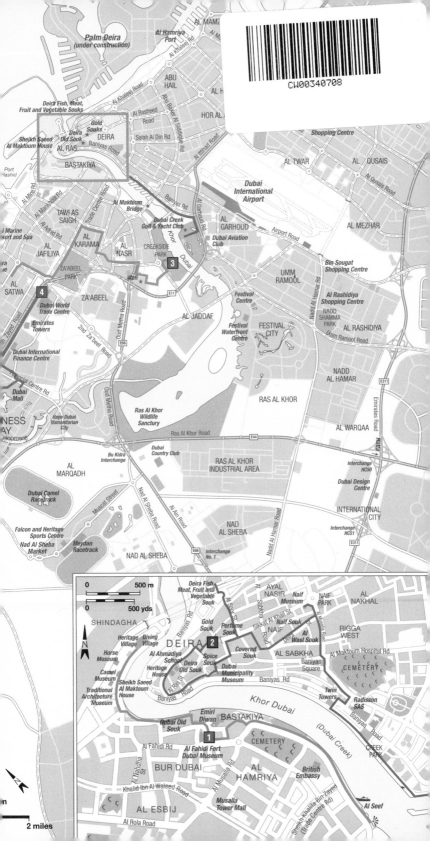

# INSIGHT GUIDES

# DUBAI
## StepbyStep

APA PUBLICATIONS **L**

Part of the Langenscheidt Publishing Group

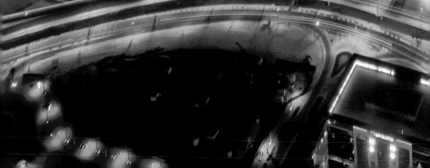

# CONTENTS

# ABOUT THIS BOOK

This *Step by Step Guide* has been produced by the editors of Insight Guides, whose books have set the standard for visual travel guides since 1970. With top-quality photography and authoritative recommendations, this guidebook brings you the very best of Dubai in a series of 15 tailor-made tours.

## WALKS AND TOURS

The tours in the book provide something to suit all budgets, tastes and trip lengths. As well as covering Dubai's classic attractions, the routes track lesser-known sights, up-and-coming areas and also excursions for those who want to extend their visit outside the city.

The tours embrace a range of interests, so whether you are a modern architecture buff, a desert-lover, a culture vulture, or want to hang out on the beach, you will find an option to suit.

We recommend that you read the whole of a tour before setting out. This should help you to familiarise yourself with the route and enable you to plan where to stop for refreshments – options are reviewed in the 'Food and Drink' boxes, recognisable by the knife-and-fork sign, on most pages.

For our pick of the walks and tours by theme, consult Recommended Tours For... *(see pp.6–7).*

## OVERVIEW

The tours are set in context by this introductory section, giving an overview of Dubai to set the scene, plus background information on food and drink, shopping, sport and beaches. A succinct history timeline in this chapter highlights the key events that have shaped Dubai over the centuries.

## DIRECTORY

Supporting the tours is a Directory chapter, comprising a user-friendly, clearly organised A-Z of practical information, our pick of where to stay while you are in the city and select restaurant and nightlife listings; the eateries described complement the more low-key cafés and restaurants that feature within the tours and offer a wider choice for evening dining.

**Above:** breathtaking Dubai.

## The Author

Gavin Thomas is a freelance UK travel writer specialising in the Gulf and South Asia. He first visited Dubai in 2005, and has since seen the Burj Khalifa emerge from a large hole in the ground, the opening of the Dubai Metro and Palm Jumeirah, and the transformation of Dubai Marina from the world's largest building site into the dazzling miniature Manhattan of today. He has written several books on the city and neighbouring emirates including the *Insight Guide Oman & The UAE,* as well as working on the *Insight Guides* to Sri Lanka and India, and writing the *Berlitz Guide Sri Lanka.* This edition builds on the previous guide written by Matt Jones.

**Margin Tips**
Shopping tips, historical facts, handy hints and information on activities help visitors to make the most of their time in Dubai.

**Feature Boxes**
Notable topics are highlighted in these special boxes.

**Key Facts Box**
This box gives details of the distance covered on the tour, plus an estimate of how long it should take. It also states where the walk/tour starts and finishes, and gives key travel information such as which days are best to do it as well as handy transport tips.

**Footers**
Those on the left-hand page give the itinerary name, plus, where relevant, a map reference; those on the right-hand page show the main attraction on the double page.

**Route Map**
Detailed cartography shows the itinerary clearly plotted with numbered dots. For more detailed mapping, see the pull-out map slotted inside the back cover.

**Food and Drink**
Recommendations of where to stop for refreshment are given in these boxes. The numbers prior to each restaurant/café name link to references in the main text. On city maps, restaurants are plotted.

The $ signs at the end of each entry reflect the approximate cost of a two-course meal for two, with a glass of house wine, where alcohol is available. These should be seen as a guide only. Price ranges, also quoted on the inside back flap for easy reference, are as follows:

| | |
|---|---|
| $$$$$ | Dhs500 and above |
| $$$$ | Dhs400–500 |
| $$$ | Dhs200–400 |
| $$ | Dhs100–200 |
| $ | Dhs100 and below |

## MODERN ARCHITECTURE

In the last 20 years Dubai has altered beyond recognition, and it now has a truly 21st-century skyline, best appreciated from Sheikh Zayed Road and Dubai Marina (tours 4 and 6).

# RECOMMENDED TOURS FOR...

### A DESERT EXPERIENCE

No visit to Dubai is complete without a trip into the desert (tour 8) and the chance to go dune bashing, quad biking or camel riding over the emirate's towering dunes.

### OFF THE BEATEN TRACK

A tour round the other emirates gives a flavour of Dubai before the oil boom (tours 12 and 13 ) and, of course, there are some lovely deserted beaches to discover here too (tour 13).

### HEDONISTIC HOTELS

Dubai has some of the biggest, glitziest and the most downright stunning hotels on the planet, enscapsulated by the iconic, 'seven-star' Burj Al Arab (tour 5).

### HIT THE BEACHES

Jumeira has some classy beach resorts (tour 5) but for some of the more off-the-beaten track beaches head out of Dubai to Fujairah (tour 13).

## TRADITIONAL DUBAI

Explore the souks, mosques and heritage houses of the old city centre during walking tours of Bur Dubai and Deira (tours 1 and 2).

## DUBAI FROM THE WATER

*Abras* are a common way to get around Dubai and for visitors a delightful way to take in views of the dramatic skyline along the Creek (tour 1); for an alternative watery experience take a trip on a sight-seeing *dhow* (tour 7).

## SHOPPING IN SOUKS

For a local shopping experience try shopping in the traditional souks of Deira (tour 2), with cut-price gold, exotic perfumes and spices, and tubs full of fragrant frankincense.

## RELIGIOUS MATTERS

Visit the vast Sheikh Zayed Grand Mosque in Abu Dhabi (tour 14), or take the informative tour of Jumeira Mosque in Dubai (tour 5).

## THRILLS AND SPILLS

Shoot around the tubes, slides and jets at Wild Wadi and Aquaventure waterparks (tours 5 and 6) or feel the thrill of Formula 1 at Yas Island's Ferrari World Abu Dhabi theme park (tour 14).

Mall of the Emirat

# OVERVIEW

An overview of Dubai's geography, customs and culture, plus illuminating background information on food and drink, shopping, sport, beaches and history.

# CITY INTRODUCTION

*Dubai is a modern Arabian metropolis, a regional hub for business and leisure and an international crossroads. This overview of its geography, culture and people provides an ideal complement to the itineraries.*

**Above:** traditional *dhow*; Burj Al Arab, viewed from above; 4x4 in the desert.

**Did You Know?**
In Arabic names, 'Bin' and 'Ibn' both mean 'son of': Mohammed Bin Rashid is Mohammed son of Rashid. 'Bint' means 'daughter of'.

Dubai's rise from unknown to household name confirms the adage that in the world of celebrity it can take 20 years to become an overnight success. In the late 1980s, few people outside the oil industry would have found this former fishing and pearling village on a map. It has now become a celebrity destination, with, among others, film star George Clooney making his movie *Syriana* here, Morgan Freeman being a regular at its annual film festival, and cricketer Andrew Flintoff now a regular with a home on the luxurious Palm Jumeirah.

The city suffered particularly badly during the credit crunch of 2008–09, with numerous articles in the international press chronicling Dubai's alleged demise, complete with the disastrous collapse of its real-estate market and incipient bankruptcy (staved off thanks to a last-minute cash injection from neighbouring Abu Dhabi). After a couple of lean years, the city is once again beginning to recapture its customary commercial verve and vibrancy.

## URBAN AREAS

Dubai is the second city (after Abu Dhabi) of the United Arab Emirates (UAE), a federation of seven sheikhdoms on the Arabian (Persian)

Gulf. The city is bounded by the sea to the west, the emirates of Sharjah and Abu Dhabi to the north and south, and by desert to the east. The city's inhospitable environment has not curtailed its ambition, and huge land-reclamation projects, oil wealth, bulldozers and seawater-desalination plants have all played a part in taming the desert.

*The Hubs*

Dubai is a linear city, stretching from north to south down the coast of the UAE for well over 20km (12 miles). The original centre of the metropolis can be found along the Creek, at the northern end of the city, flanked by the communities of Shindagha, Bur Dubai and Deira. The modern city has since expanded gradually southwards from here, spreading down the Jumeira coast and the parallel Sheikh Zayed Road before reaching the huge new Downtown Dubai development, roughly at the midpoint of the modern city. South of here development continues, eventually reaching the huge new Dubai Marina.

## THE DESERT

Dubai is the capital of the emirate of Dubai, which covers some 3,900 sq

km (1,506 miles). While the city itself is flat, the topography inland consists of rolling dunes and the foothills of the Hajar Mountains. Climbing to a peak of 2,000m (6,560ft), the Hajar range separates Dubai from the Arabian Gulf – just over an hour's drive from the city. The desert is a playground for residents with four-wheel drive vehicles, motorbikes and quads; for visitors, an off-road desert safari with a local tour operator is a must. The UAE's largest desert conservation reserve centres around the luxury Al Maha Desert Resort and Spa, where rare Arabian oryx roam free.

## CLIMATE

Summers in Dubai are hot and humid. From May to September daytime temperatures rarely fall below 40°C (104°F), with humidity up to 90 per cent. From October to April, the weather resembles an extremely good European summer, with temperatures hovering around 30°C (mid-80s°F) and with little or no humidity. Evenings can feel chilly in January and February, when sweaters may be required.

### Rainfall

Annual rainfall is minimal (an average of 42mm/1.5in), but downpours can

Above from far left: the Emirates Towers dominate the Sheikh Zayed Road skyline; tiled dome in the Persian court in Ibn Battuta Mall; local man; the desert.

Below: Arab men having coffee together.

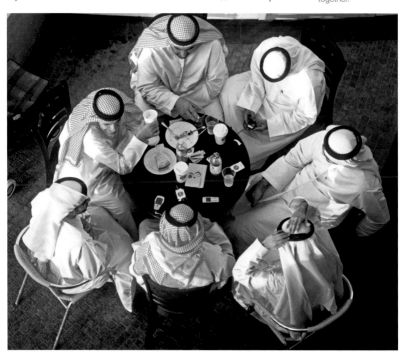

**Above from left:** high-rise city skyline; camel; palm tree; spectacular interior of the Burj Al Arab.

occur between November and March; when it rains, it pours, so if you plan to explore a *wadi* (dry river bed), check that it is not raining in the mountains, otherwise you could be caught in a flood. Inland, Hatta is a cool retreat from the more humid coast.

## WHEN TO GO

November to April is when the climate is at its best. It is then that Dubai's lively sports and social scenes come to life. However, before you book, it is advisable to check when the holy month of Ramadan falls, as there will be restrictions on music and nightlife.

Visiting during the scorching summer months is less appealing, although on the plus side rates at many of the city's upmarket hotels and resorts can fall dramatically.

## POPULATION

Dubai's population had reached almost 1.9 million in 2010, while the population of the UAE as a whole is one of the fastest-growing in the Arab world, hovering close to the five million mark. Dubai is also one of the world's most multicultural cities. Over 90 per cent of residents are expatriates, ranging from low-wage Indian and Pakistani construction workers and Filipino waitresses through to more affluent expat Arabs from the Levant and North Africa, as well as a sizeable community of European and North American professionals. Emiratis in Dubai thus find themselves in the curious position of being virtual foreigners in their own city, and it's possible to visit Dubai and meet very few Emirati nationals except for those at airport immigration and the tourist information counters in malls.

### The Bedu

One of the oldest tribespeople in the world, the Bedu (Bedouin) were

**Below:** the more traditional side of Dubai.

once nomadic herdsmen, living off the products of their animals. Today, however, Bedu culture and lifestyle are under threat from the modernisation that oil wealth has brought to the Emirates.

### National Dress

UAE national dress is worn in the workplace, at home and when out and about. The men's white, floor-length robe is known as the *kandoora* or *dishdasha*. The cloth headdress, which can be white or red-and-white check, is a *gutra*, secured by a

stiff black cord known as an *agal*, with which their Bedu ancestors hobbled their camels' legs – although among young men baseball caps are increasingly replacing the *gutra* and *agal*.

The most visible items of women's clothing are the floor-length black cloak, the *abaya*, and headscarf, called a *sheyla*. Older women may be seen wearing the stiff gold and lacquer face mask known as a *burqa*, though this is becoming less common. Children often dress in Western-style clothes.

**Multilingual Dubai**
Given the number of different nationalities resident in Dubai – upwards of 180 – you are as likely to hear Hindi, Urdu, Malayalam and Tagalog as Arabic. While Arabic is the UAE's official language, English is widely spoken and used for everyday contact between the various groups.

# Parks and Reserves

For such a built-up city, Dubai is surprisingly well-provided with parks. Most are open from 8am until well after dark; most charge small entrance fees. Perhaps the best park within the city limits is the expansive Creekside Park (see p.43; daily 8am–10.30pm). Other green spaces include Safa Park (Sat–Thur 8am–11pm, Fri 8am–11.30pm), between southern Jumeira and Sheikh Zayed Road, a favourite with joggers and local youngsters drawn by its fairground attractions. The attractive Al Mamzar Park (see p.43) is another favourite thanks to its fine stretches of beach and expansive parkland areas.

The low-key Ras Al Khor Wildlife Sanctuary (Sat–Thur 9am–4pm; free; www.wildlife.ae), at the end of the Creek, south of the Festival Centre development, is an important stopover on winter migratory routes from East Africa to West Asia (almost 70 different species have been spotted here). It is best known for its flocks of bright pink flamingoes – one of Dubai's most surreal sights. There are two hides from which you can spot birdlife (free binoculars are provided). The better one is on the western side of the sanctuary (beside the E66 Highway just north of the junction with the Hatta Road). The second is on the south side of the sanctuary, on the north side of the Hatta Road (you'll need to do an 8km loop back around to the correct side of the highway).

# FOOD AND DRINK

*From simple Emirati dishes with lamb or fish to colourful Moroccan feasts, Dubai offers visitors the Arab world on a plate. But this cosmopolitan city is also a culinary melting pot that caters for diverse international tastes.*

**Above:** Japengo Café; dates; Al Nafoorah.

**Zero Tolerance**
Dubai has a zero-tolerance approach to drink driving. The penalty for being found with the smallest amount of alcohol in your blood can be a month in jail, with more severe penalties for causing death through drink driving. The bottom line is that if you're going to drink alcohol, take a taxi.

Dubai's local eating out guides bulge with details of an expanding number of restaurants serving authentic cuisine from all over the world. From alfresco Lebanese eateries to hip New Zealand-owned cafés and no-frills sushi bars with racks of Manga comics near the entrance and salarymen at the counter, Dubai offers rich pickings for tastebud tourists. It may be a Muslim society, but visitors will find a liberal attitude to the sale of pork and alcohol.

## WORLD-CLASS CUISINE

For dedicated diners, whether carnivorous or vegetarian, Dubai has all the ingredients for memorable meals, from delicious *shawarmas* (meat cooked on a vertical spit and served with garlic paste in Arabic bread) sold by street vendors to fine dining in luxury hotels.

Given the amount of money in the emirate and the increasingly cosmopolitan nature of both its inhabitants and visitors, it is little surprise that Dubai has developed into a regional centre for world-class cuisine. In 2001 British celebrity chef Gordon Ramsay chose Dubai for Verre *(see p.115)*, his first restaurant outside the UK. Other celebrity restaurateurs include India's Sanjeev Kapoor, who has Khazana at Al Nasr Leisureland *(see p.116)*, and

Bollywood legend Asha Bhosle, who owns Asha's at Wafi.

## WHERE TO EAT

Dubai's best restaurants are located in hotels that are vibrant social centres for nationals, expatriates and visitors alike. Those that have a number of different food outlets and bars feel like mini-neighbourhoods through which you can stroll in air-conditioned comfort. And in contrast to the majority of 'high street' and mall restaurants, all hotels are licensed to sell alcohol.

For a combination of excellent food and pitch-perfect ambience, consider the seafood restaurants Al Mahara *(see p.117)* at Burj Al Arab and Pierchic *(see p.119)* at Al Qasr, Zheng He's Chinese *(see p.119)* at Mina A'Salam and the European restaurants Vu's *(see p.117)* at Emirates Towers and Spectrum On One *(see p.117)* at the Fairmont. For Arabic food, try the Lebanese restaurant Al Qasr *(see p.118)* at Dubai Marine Beach Resort (not to be confused with the hotel of the same name) or Emirates Towers' Al Nafoorah *(see p.117)*.

### Outside the Hotels
Away from hotels, popular Lebanese chains such as Beirut, Automatic and

Zaatar W Zeit offer excellent value for money. Other popular eateries include the funky Dutch-owned More bistro, including one in Al Marooj complex off Sheikh Zayed Road (there's another one in Garhoud, *see p.116*) and The Lime Tree Café *(see p.58)* on Jumeirah Road. For waterfront dining, choose The Boardwalk at Dubai Creek Golf & Yacht Club *(see p.38)* or any of the outlets overlooking the canals in the Madinat Jumeirah resort. The atmospheric Bastakiah Nights *(see p.114)* offers Iranian and Arabic food in a restored house in historic Bastakiya near Dubai Creek. If you need fuel after hours of sightseeing or shopping, every mall has at least one food court.

## TIMING AND PAYMENT

Residents tend to dine late at night, so for a good atmosphere plan dinner from around 9pm. If you're heading for a hotel venue, book in advance. Major credit and debit cards are widely accepted, although smaller, cheaper places may only accept cash.

## ARABIC CUISINE

In the main, for Arabic food read Lebanese. Mezze – small dishes and dips – are the Middle East's equivalent of tapas. Staple mezze scooped up with flat Arabic bread are: *hummus* (a chickpea paste with olive oil, garlic and lemon juice); *tabbouleh* (a herb salad with bulgar wheat); *fattoush* (a finely chopped tomato, cucumber and lettuce salad); *mutabel* (similar to hummus but

made with smoked eggplant); and *falafel* (fried chickpea patties). Mezze are usually followed by a main course such as grilled meat, but are a satisfying meal in themselves.

### Regional Dishes

Emirati food derives from simple Bedu fare and consists mainly of fish, chicken and lamb served as kebabs or biriani-style with rice. *Matchbous* is spiced lamb with rice, *hareis* is slow-cooked wheat and lamb, and *fareed* is a meat and vegetable stew poured over thin bread. Flavourings include cumin, cardamom and coriander. Khan Murjan Restaurant *(see p.45)* and Al Makan *(see p.58)* offer local food.

### Desserts

Arabic desserts typically feature nuts, syrup and fresh cream. Popular puddings include *Umm Ali* ('Mother of Ali'), a bread and butter pudding with sultanas and coconut, topped with nuts, and *Kashta*, clotted cream topped with pistachio, pine seeds and honey.

## DRINKS

Delicious fresh juices are available in Arabic restaurants. Traditional Arabian coffee *(kahwa)* is flavoured with cardamom and served in small, handleless cups. Thick Turkish coffee is more commonly served in restaurants. If you don't like your coffee sweet, ask for 'medium sweet' *(wasat)* or 'without sugar' *(bidoon sukkar)*. Arabic-style tea, also served sweet, is without milk and flavoured with cardamom or mint.

**Above from far left:**
Fruit and Vegetable Souk; tea-seller; Deira Fish Souk; cocktails at the luxury Dusit Dubai hotel.

**Ramadan Rules**
Whatever your religion, it is illegal to eat in public in daylight during the holy month of Ramadan, when Muslims abstain from food and drink from sunrise to sunset. Some restaurants open for lunch but screen off their eating areas. Although pork and alcohol are not consumed by Muslims, several hotel restaurants use them as ingredients in certain dishes. These will be highlighted with a symbol on the menu.

# SHOPPING

*For many visitors, Dubai's various attractions – from the cultural to the rest-and-recreation variety – are mere sideshows to the main event: its shops. For dedicated shoppers, Dubai is the proverbial paradise.*

**Above:** wide range of wares from Cartier to shisha pipes.

Selling Dubai
World-famous Dubai Duty Free has led the way in terms of promoting the city on the international stage, thanks to its sponsorship of snooker, tennis, horse racing and powerboating. But selling Dubai goes hand in hand with trading in gold, perfumes and a whole lot more besides at Dubai International Airport. With record annual sales of $1.27 billion in 2010, Dubai Duty Free is one of the world's largest airport retailers.

Shopping in Dubai takes two forms. The first is in the old-fashioned souks of Deira and Bur Dubai, where you'll find traditional Arabian produce and artefacts – gold, spices, perfumes – lined up for sale in myriad shoe-box shops. Prices are generally cheap, although bargaining is essential. The second is in the city's vast array of modern malls, which offer popular brands, designer fashions and fabulously expensive watches and jewellery aplenty – while the eye-popping design of some malls makes them virtual tourist attractions in their own right.

Madinat Jumeirah *(see p.59)* and Khan Murjan *(see p.45)* are the best.

*Other Souks*

Further afield, Sharjah's Blue Souk is one of the best places to buy carpets from Iran and Pakistan and also has a wide selection of 'antiques', including *khanjars* which are short, curved decorative daggers traditionally tucked into men's trousers at the waist.

The best time to shop at souks is in the morning and late afternoon to evening; they are closed in the early afternoon and Friday mornings.

## SOUKS

*The Main Souks*

For bargains and a vibrant atmosphere, nothing beats the traditional souks. The most famous is Deira's Gold Souk, one of the cheapest places in the world to buy the precious metal, while the nearby Spice and Perfume souks stock a wide range of unusual spices and flowery scents (or create your own). Across the Creek in Bur Dubai, the Old Souk is the place to head for cheap fabrics and cheesy souvenirs. Also worth exploring are the city's modern souks, replica bazaars built in faux-Arabian style, often with spectacular décor – Souk

## MALLS

For air-conditioned comfort, convenient access and, in several cases, the wow factor, try Dubai's malls. All have gold and jewellery stores that may satisfy you in the unlikely event the Gold Souk does not. Most open 10am–10pm, and later during the holidays and Ramadan.

*Major malls*

Far and away the biggest mall in the city is the mighty Dubai Mall *(see p.51)*, the world's largest, while the huge Mall of the Emirates, near Interchange 4 on Sheikh Zayed Road, is another top shopping destination,

home to a branch of the upmarket department store Harvey Nichols, a large Arabian Treasures section for souvenirs and carpets, as well as surreal views over the indoor ski slopes of Ski Dubai, covered in artificial snow.

The more modest Deira City Centre is a perennial favourite, but vying with Mall of the Emirates as Dubai's swankiest shopping destination are the stately BurJuman Centre, home to Saks Fifth Avenue, and the Egyptian-themed Wafi *(see p.44)*, both on the Bur Dubai side of the Creek. The zany Ibn Battuta Mall *(see p.62)* is also worth a visit for its outlandish décor, as is the chintzy Italian-style Mercato Mall *(see p.57)*.

## ON THE STREET

Dubai has few open-air 'high streets'. Deira's Al Riqqa Road is a pleasant avenue of boutiques, while the parallel Maktoum Road's boutiques include Gianni Versace, Dolce & Gabbana and Cartier. In Satwa, there are boutiques dotted along Al Dhiyafah Road.

*Electronics, Textiles and Crafts*
For electronic goods and watches, head for Al Fahidi Street in Bur Dubai. The port end of Khalid Bin Al Waleed Road in Bur Dubai is the place for computers and software.

If you want colourful silks or textiles, check out the many small shops in the Old Souk and along Al Fahidi Street in Bur Dubai, while cheap clothes shops and tailors can be found in Karama.

For local artwork, visit the small galleries that have sprung up around Bastakiya, in The Gate building on Sheikh Zayed Road *(see p.50)* and in Al Quoz industrial area off Sheikh Zayed Road. The Covent Garden Market *(see p.61)* at The Walk, Jumeirah Beach Residence, Dubai Marina, is also good.

## BARGAINING

Don't assume that because of Dubai's tax-free reputation, everything here is cheaper than elsewhere in the world. You can bargain for deals in the souks, but not in malls, except perhaps when buying carpets or large souvenirs, and you are more likely to get a large discount with cash. The trick is to disguise your interest in the item you really want, then offer half of what you're prepared to pay, and take it from there.

# SPORT

*Dubai has gained an international reputation for world-class sporting events, and visitors can watch the stars of golf, tennis, rugby, horse racing and other major sports here at various times of the year.*

**Olympic Hopeful**
The world's first purpose-built city for sport, Dubai Sports City, is a feature of the massive Dubailand development near Emirates Road. It now serves as the home for the Ernie Els Golf Club, Dubai Autodrome and Dubai Cricket Stadium. Locals hope it will one day host the Olympic Games.

Dubai has a surprisingly extensive range of top-class sporting events, including the world's richest horse race, leading golf, tennis and rugby tournaments and international cricket fixtures, while Abu Dhabi hosts the season-ending Formula 1 Grand Prix. Tickets for all events are surprisingly affordable and fairly easy to get, by European and North American standards, though all events are extremely popular, and it's a good idea to reserve tickets as far in advance as possible.

## HORSE RACING

The spectacular new Meydan Racecourse is the prime venue for horse racing in the UAE – a state-of-the-art venue including a strikingly modern stadium, with room for 60,000 spectators, and a 2.4km turf track.

The racing season is held during the cooler winter months from November to March, culminating in the prestigious Dubai World Cup, the world's richest horse race with prize money of $10 million. Race-meets are also a major feature on the city's social calendar, attracting a lively crowd of Emiratis and expats, although no betting is allowed.

## GOLF

Dubai has a superb selection of golf courses, including the Emirates Golf Club, the nearby Montgomerie at Emirates Hills, the Four Seasons' Al Badia course at Dubai Festival City, the Arabian Ranches' desert course in Dubailand, the Els Club in Dubai Sports City in Dubailand, and Dubai Creek Golf & Yacht Club. The Emirates Golf Club is home to the men's Dubai Desert Classic, part of the European Tour, held annually in November and attracting an elite international field – past winners have included Ernie Els, Colin Montgomerie, Rory McIlroy and Tiger Woods. The Dubai Ladies Masters is also held here.

## TENNIS

The Dubai Tennis Chamionship (late Feb/early March; www.dubaitennis championships.com) is an established fixture on the men's and women's singles circuit – past winners have included Venus Williams, Justine Henin, Caroline Wozniacki, Andy Roddick, Rafael Nadal, Novak Djokovic (who has won the last three tournaments) and Roger Federer, who has won the men's event four times.

## RUGBY

The Dubai Rugby Sevens (www.dubairugby7s.com) is part of the International Rugby Board (IRB) Sevens World Series. The three-day tournament at The Sevens stadium on the edge of the city on the road to Al Ain is contested by the world's best teams every December – and is accompanied by some of the city's most riotous partying.

## CRICKET

The 25,000-seater cricket stadium at Dubai Sports City (www.dubaisports city.ae) in Dubailand hosts occasional one-day and Twenty20 internationals between leading teams – England, Australia, New Zealand and Pakistan have all played here in past years.

## CARS, BIKES AND BOATS

The leading regional motorsports event is the season-ending Formula 1 Etihad Airways Abu Dhabi Grand Prix, held at Yas Island *(see p.91)* in mid-November. The Abu Dhabi Desert Challenge, a FIA-sanctioned car and motorbike rally, also takes place in November in the deserts around Abu Dhabi. On road, the racetrack at Dubai Autodrome in Dubailand hosts various other international events through the year. On the water, the final rounds of the UIM Class One World Offshore powerboat championships take place off Le Meridien Mina Seyahi in late October/early November. The Dubai-based Victory team are local favourites.

## CAMEL RACING

The traditional local pasttime of camel racing is enduringly popular in Dubai, although the famous old camel race-course in Nad al Sheba closed in 2009, and meets are now held at Al Lisaili Race Track (050-658 8528), some 40km from Dubai off exit 37 along the road to Al Ain. Races are held during the cooler winter months from September to May; most start early in the morning (around 6am). Call the racetrack for details of events.

**Above from far left:** buggies at the Montgomerie golf course; Camel racing.

## Home Fixtures

Swedish golfer Henrik Stenson didn't have far to travel with his trophy when won the Dubai Desert Classic in 2007; his home is in Emirates Hills, just a five-minute drive from Emirates Golf Club. Danish golfer Thomas Bjorn also lives in Dubai, while cricketer Andrew Flintoff also owns a villa on Palm Jumeirah. The city is also a winter base for Swiss tennis ace Roger Federer, who has a pad at Dubai Marina and practises on the courts of the luxury Al Qasr hotel when he's in town. Dubai is even home to the International Cricket Council (ICC), which moved to the city in 2005 after 96 years at Lord's cricket ground in London.

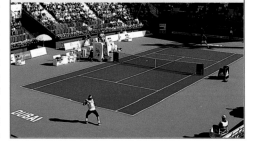

# BEACHES

*Dubai's beaches are clean, safe and seldom overcrowded. With the exception of Al Mamzar Beach Park (on the border with Sharjah), most are located in the southern end of the city, while further stretches of sand are appearing around the fringes of Palm Jumeirah as land-reclamation progresses.*

**Above:** strolling along the beach; lifeguards on watch.

**Statistics**
Dubai's natural coastline is 72km (45 miles) long, but land reclamation projects are extending it by an incredible 1,500km (932 miles), which is longer than the natural coastline of the entire UAE.

Dubai's Arabian Gulf coastline, with its palm-fringed golden sands and azure waters, is one of the city's major draws, although the city doesn't boast a picturesque, Mediterranean-style coast with sweeping bays and varying topography – here the Gulf coastline is straight and flat (if you want a mountain backdrop for your swim, head for the UAE's more rugged Arabian Sea coast); and the only elevated views are from hotel rooms and restaurants. The coast isn't exactly unspoilt, either, both on the natural coastline and on the various land reclamation projects that are underway all the way to the emirate's boundary with Abu Dhabi.

These caveats aside, most beaches have been carefully manicured, with trees, lawns or breakwaters added to enhance their appeal, and are swept by tractors first thing in the morning. They certainly deliver the rest and relaxation promised in tourist brochures and holidaymaker's most basic requirements: sun, sand and sea.

## KEY POINTS

Before you head off to the beach, there are just a few important things to note. There's a strong undertow and currents along the coast, even in the shallows, and drownings are not uncommon, so beware. Always swim within sight of a lifeguard and never when the red flag is flying. One option is to save the beach for basking and ball games and opt to swim in a beachside pool instead.

In terms of cultural considerations, restrictions are minimal – normal beachwear is acceptable, for example – but women should be aware that topless bathing is a strict no-no, and no one should walk around in bathing costumes away from the beach. Other considerations include special days for women and young children only, and, during Ramadan, changes in opening times of the beach parks and the absence of refreshments.

## HOTEL BEACHES

All the hotels in the Dubai Marina – including the Sheraton Jumeirah Beach, the Hilton Dubai Jumeirah, the Habtoor Grand, the Ritz-Carlton Dubai, Le Meridien Mina Seyahi, the Jumeirah Beach Hotel and the opulent One&Only Royal Mirage – have their own beaches. If you aren't a guest, all of these hotels will allow you to use their beach facilities on a daily basis, albeit at often extortionate rates (from Dhs100 and upwards).

## PUBLIC BEACHES

A much cheaper alternative is to visit one of Dubai's public beaches, which, with their mix of nationalities and wide range of income groups, are more representative of the city. On weekends and public holidays these beaches and beach parks become focal points for popular events such as family barbecues and kite-flying festivals.

*Popular public beaches*

The best public beach in the city is at the Jumeira Beach Park (see p.57; daily 7am–10.30pm, Mon women and boys aged up to 4 only; Dhs5), which boasts a gorgeous swathe of white sand with lifeguards, backed by attractive parkland with barbecues, cafés and children's play areas.

There's a further stretch of fine beach right next door at the new **Shoreside complex** (www.shoreside. ae), although at a much higher admission price – more like an upmarket resort than a public beach,

with loungers, parasols and an attractive restaurant. Various watersports are also available, along with a range of children's activities. Entrance for two people costs Dhs250 (including Dhs75 food and drink) on weekdays, or a very pricey Dhs450 (including Dhs100 food and drink) on Friday and Saturday; children cost Dhs100 (Fri-Sat Dhs175).

A cheaper option is Al Mamzar Park (daily 8am–11pm; Dhs5), on the north side of Deira close to the border with Sharjah, which has a string of sandy coves and extensive parkland, plus fine views of Sharjah over the lagoon.

Free beaches (open 24hr) include the rather windswept Jumeira Public Beach (also known as 'Russian Beach') in northern Jumeira near the Dubai Marine Beach Resort & Spa and the pleasant Umm Suqeim beach, right next to the Burj Al Arab. The strip of public beach in Dubai Marina *(see p.61)* is another attractive option, with loads of sand backdropped by the futuristic high-rise Marina skyline.

**Above from far left:** catching up on the news on Jumeira Public Beach; Jumeira Beach Park; Emiratis playing football on the beach; mother and daughter feeding the seagulls on a public beach in Jumeira.

**Midnight Dips**
If you go for a midnight dip you may see the luminescence of microscopic sea creatures around you – they give off a blue-green light when the water is disturbed.

## Water Parks

Dubai's superb, state-of-the-art water parks are Wild Wadi Water Park (next to the Jumeirah Beach Hotel; tel: 04 438 4444; daily Sept–Oct, Mar–May 10am–7pm, Nov–Feb 11am–6pm, Jun–Aug 11am–8pm; www.wildwadi.com), and Aquaventure, at Atlantis on Palm Jumeirah (daily 10am–sunset; tel: 04 426 0000; www.atlantisthepalm.com). Both boast watery thrills and spills, ranging from lazy rivers and wave pools for younger kids through to water slides and power jets, plus the stomach-churning Jumeirah Sceirah drops you 33m (108ft) at speeds of up to 80kph (50mph), and the Leap of Faith at Aquavenutre which dumps you down a near-verticle, 27m (89ft) long slide into a lagoon full of sharks.

# HISTORY: KEY DATES

*An introduction to the region, from fishing village to economic powerhouse, via the dawn of Islam, the arrival of European powers and the rise of the Maktoum dynasty.*

**Above:** the preserved ruins of an ancient settlement near Hatta and Fossil Rock; defensive watchtower in the walls of the Al Hosn Palace in Abu Dhabi.

**National Day**
The UAE's National Day holiday on 2 December begins four days of festivities celebrating the founding of the federation in 1971. At heritage venues in Dubai, look out for special exhibitions, cultural activities and performances of the traditional men's Ayyalah battle dance.

## PRE-ISLAM

| | |
|---|---|
| *c*.5000 BC | Stone Age settlements are established on the Arabian Gulf coast and in the Hajar Mountains. |
| 2700–2000 BC | A Bronze Age settlement is established at Al Sufouh, Dubai. |
| 1st century BC | An Iron Age village is established at Al Ghusais, Dubai. |
| 4th century AD | Christianity arrives in Bet Mazunaye, an area corresponding to the modern UAE and northern Oman. |
| 6th century | The Sassanids establish a trading post in Jumeira. Aramaic is the region's lingua franca. |
| *c*.632–5 | The Battle of Dibba marks the dawn of the Islamic era on the Arabian peninsula. Arabic replaces Aramaic. |

## EUROPEAN INTEREST

| | |
|---|---|
| 16th century | Portuguese imperialists recognise the Arabian coast's strategic importance en route to India's riches. |
| 1580 | The earliest surviving written reference to 'Dibei' is made by Venetian jeweller Gasparo Balbi. |
| 1793 | Dubai, a fishing and pearling village of 1,200 people, is a dependency of Abu Dhabi. |
| 1822 | A British treaty with Mohammed Bin Hazza is the first recognition on paper that Dubai is a separate entity to more powerful Abu Dhabi and Sharjah. |
| 1833 | Maktoum Bin Buti Al Maktoum and 800 members of the Bani Yas tribe arrive in Shindagha from Abu Dhabi. Maktoum rule. |
| 1853 | The Perpetual Treaty of Maritime Truce between Britain and local sheikhs safeguards British sea trade with India. The region becomes known as the 'Trucial Coast'. |
| 1894 | Sheikh Maktoum Bin Hasher uses tax concessions to encourage foreign merchants to settle in Dubai. |
| 1902 | Increased customs duties in the Persian port of Lingah prompt more foreign traders to migrate to Dubai's free-trade zone. |

| 1929 | Wall Street crash causes pearl prices to fall. The subsequent introduction of the Japanese cultured pearl sounds the industry's death knell and plunges Dubai into an economic depression. |

## POST-WORLD WAR II

| 1951 | Britain establishes the Trucial Oman Scouts to keep order and support oil exploration in the interior. |
| 1958 | Sheikh Rashid Bin Saeed Al Maktoum, the 'father of modern Dubai', becomes ruler. |
| 1966 | Oil is discovered in Dubai. Exports begin within three years. |
| 1967 | The population of Dubai reaches 59,000. |
| 1971 | The United Arab Emirates (UAE) is established with Abu Dhabi ruler Sheikh Zayed Bin Sultan Al Nahyan as President and Dubai's Sheikh Rashid as Vice President. |
| 1985 | Dubai-based airline Emirates is established. |

## A NEW ERA

| 1990 | Sheikh Rashid dies. He is succeeded by his son Sheikh Maktoum Bin Rashid Al Maktoum. |
| 1994 | Sheikh Maktoum's brother, Sheikh Mohammed Bin Rashid Al Maktoum, is made Crown Prince of Dubai. |
| 1996 | The Dubai Strategic Plan indicates that oil will run out by 2010; plans are made to diversify the economy. The Dubai World Cup, the world's richest horse race, is run for the first time at Nad Al Sheba Racecourse. Also the first Dubai Shopping Festival. |
| 2001 | Following a boom in tourism work begins on Palm Jumeirah, and The Palm, Jebel Ali, two man-made, palm-shaped islands. |
| 2002 | The government announces 100 percent freehold ownership for non-nationals, unleashing a construction boom. |
| 2004 | Sheikh Zayed, the founder and President of the UAE, dies at the age of 86. His son Sheikh Khalifa becomes President. |
| 2006 | Sheikh Maktoum dies aged 62. His brother Sheikh Mohammed succeeds him as Ruler of Dubai and Prime Minister of the UAE. Population of Dubai passes 1.4 million. |
| 2007 | Burj Khalifa becomes the world's tallest building on 21 July, passing the 509m (1,670ft) record set by Taipei 101. |
| 2008 | The credit crunch hits Dubai, pushing the emirate to the brink of bankruptcy and stalling many major construction projects. |
| 2010 | Opening of the Burj Khalifa. |

**Above from far left:** men smoking 'shisha' water pipes in a coffee shop in a Dubai souk; ultra-modern key-pad for the myriad floors in a Dubai skyscraper.

**The Maktoums**
The Maktoum family has ruled Dubai since 1833. The current ruler, Sheikh Mohammed Bin Rashid Al Maktoum, is also Vice President and Prime Minister of the UAE. It is the visionary Sheikh Mohammed who is credited for transforming Dubai from an oil-based economy to a centre for international commerce and global dialogue. Former US Secretary of State Madeleine Albright called Dubai a 'Davos with sand instead of snow'.

# WALKS AND TOURS

# BUR DUBAI

*This leisurely walking tour begins with a visit to the excellent Dubai Museum, followed by a stroll through Bur Dubai's Old Souk and the fine old traditional districts of Shindagha and Bastakiya, before continuing down the waterside to admire the modern buildings lining the Creek.*

**DISTANCE** 4.5km (3 miles)
**TIME** A full day
**START** Dubai Museum, Bur Dubai
**END** Al Seef Abra Station, Bur Dubai
**POINTS TO NOTE**
Take a taxi to the starting point of this walking tour.

**Below:** loading a cargo *dhow* on Dubai Creek's Deira quayside.

Dubai has developed spectacularly in the past 50 years. What was once a small fishing and trading community has become a commercial and leisure hub with towering concrete, metal-and-glass structures. A large proportion of the new prosperity has been reinvested on the wide crescent of Dubai Creek. Separating Deira from Bur Dubai, and cutting through the historic heart of a now sprawling metropolis, the Creek is much changed from the 1940s when British flying boats touched down here en route to Australia.

## DUBAI OLD SOUK AND AROUND

*Al Fahidi Fort and Dubai Museum*
Right in the heart of Bur Dubai lies the quaint **Al Fahidi Fort ❶**. This is the oldest surviving structure in the city, built between 1787 and 1799 to guard the landward approach to town. The fortress originally served as the ruler's residence and seat of government; it also provided a refuge for Dubai's inhabitants in the event of attack, whilst also serving as the city jail. The building itself – a simple, square, high-walled compound with corner towers covered in

sun-baked plaster – is an arresting, if rather care-worn, sight among the surrounding modern apartment blocks and office buildings. On the square beside it stands a stunning replica of the wooden pearling *dhows* that were used in the 18th and 19th centuries.

Since 1971, the fort has housed the **Dubai Museum** (tel: 04 353 1862; www.dubaitourism.ae; Sat–Thur 8.30am–8.30pm, Fri 2.30–8.30pm; charge). A visit to the museum is rewarding; most of the exhibits are displayed in a sequence of underground galleries, with excellent displays covering every aspect of traditional life in the city including an old-fashioned souk, complete with life-size shops and mannequins, plus extensive finds from the archaeological sites at Al Qusais and Jumeira, dating back to the Iron Age and 6th century.

## Juma Grand Mosque

Immediately behind the museum stands the **Juma Grand Mosque ❷** (closed to non-Muslims). This is one of the oldest mosques in Dubai (dating back to 1900, although it was rebuilt in 1998), and also boasts the city's tallest minaret (70m/231ft), nine large domes, 45 small domes and space for 1,200 worshippers. You can take a peek inside from the doorway, but, unless you are a Muslim, don't venture in.

**Above from far left:**
Bastakiya wind tower;
local man;
architectural detail
on a doorway;
Dubai Creek, with
cargo *dhows* and
*abras* in view.

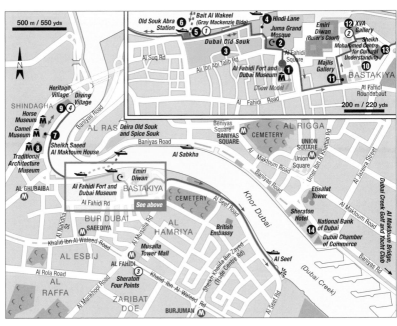

### On the Water

Most tour operators in the city offer **dhow** dinner cruises along the Creek aboard various vessels (see p.67). Two of the most popular are the traditional Al Mansour Dhow, operated by the Radisson Blu hotel in Deira (tel: 04 205 7333) and the more contemporary Bateaux Dubai (04 399 4994, www.jebelali-international.com). The Danat Dubai (www.danatdubai cruises.com; tel: 04 351 1117), a modern sightseeing and dining boat, is anchored at the junction of Al Seef Road and Sheikh Khalifa Bin Zayed/ Trade Centre Road. The same company offers a more sedate ride aboard a wooden dhow..

### Dubai Old Souk

Turning left here and heading down any of the various little alleyways brings you into **Dubai Old Souk ❸** (Sat–Thur 10am–1pm & 4–10pm, Fri 4–10pm). This is the most attractive of all Dubai's souks, with dozens of little shops lined up in old coral-and-stone buildings under a high wooden roof; most sell cheap clothes and textiles, while a few offer souvenirs and a few antique handicrafts. Here and there the shops open up to reveal glorious views of the Creek, dotted with chuntering *abras* and old wooden *dhows*, with the wind-towered souks of Deira beyond.

At the end of the souk, behind the Grand Mosque, lies the narrow alleyway known as '**Hindi Lane**' ❹, with shops selling Indian religious paraphernalia – flower garlands, portraits and horoscopes – and a tiny Hindu-cum-Sikh temple halfway along, then up the stairs on your left.

### Gray Mackenzie Building

Overlooking the *abra* station is the old, two-storey **Gray Mackenzie Building** ❺ (also known as the 'Bait Al Wakeel'), constructed in 1932. This, the first purpose-built office building in Dubai, was the initial base for the city's British agencies and trade missions. It now houses **Bait Al Wakeel,** see ⑪① restaurant by the water.

### Dubai Old Souk Abra Station

Right next to the northern entrance to the Dubai Old Souk lies the **Old Souk Abra Station ❻**, which links up with Al Sabkha Abra Station *(see p.38)* in Deira. This is a hive of activity most days, with dozens of small boats jostling for custom at the pontoons.

### ABRA RIDE

While you're here, it's worth (if you haven't already been on one) hopping aboard an *abra* at the station and making the wonderful five-minute ride across the Creek. This costs just one *dirham* per person per trip, but could well be one of the highlights of your visit to Dubai. The views from the water of both sides of the Creek are magnificent – a wonderful blend of traditional and modern, with wind-towers and minarets jostling for elbow-room with glass-fronted high-rises and huge neon signs. The boat ride itself is equally memorable, scrunched up almost at water level amidst a cosmopolitan crowd of fellow passengers who usually offer a good cross-section of Dubai society, from Pakistani expat labourers through to robed Emiratis and tanned tourists.

### SHINDAGHA

Continuing past Bur Dubai Abra Station, a breezy promenade leads along the waterfront into the historic Creekside district of Shindagha, with stunning views up-river towards the *abra* stations and the jumble of Creek-side buildings and minarets.

### Al Maktoums

It was here, too, that 800 members of the Al Bu Falasah sub-section of the Bani Yas tribe settled after seceding from Abu Dhabi in 1833. Led by Sheikh Maktoum Bin Buti and Sheikh Obaid Bin Saeed Bin Rashid, the Bani Yas influx transformed the politics of a community that had numbered around 1,200 people before their arrival. Maktoum became its new ruler, establishing at Shindagha the Al Maktoum dynasty that rules Dubai to this day.

### Sheikh Saeed Al Maktoum House

A 5–10min walk brings you to **Sheikh Saeed Al Maktoum House** ❼ (tel: 04 393 7139; Sat–Thur 8am–8.30pm; Fri 3–9.30pm; charge). The former home of the ruling Maktoum family, the house was built in 1896 for Sheikh Maktoum Bin Hasher Al Maktoum but now named after his successor Sheikh Saeed, who ruled the emirate from 1912 to 1958. Comprehensively restored between 1984 and 1986, this two-storey structure, built from coral stone and covered in lime and sand-coloured plaster, is an impressive example of late 19th-century Emirati architecture, with elegant arched doorways, carved trellis and four wind towers.

The house is now home to one of Dubai's most interesting museums, documenting the social, cultural, educational and religious history of the emirate, although the undoubted highlight is the fascinating collection of old photographs from the 1940s to 1960s charting the city's transformation from modest town to modern metropolis.

### Traditional Architecture, Horse and Camel museums

Immediately to the south, the **Traditional Architecture Museum** ❽ (daily, except Fri, 7am–7pm; free), occupies another fine old wind-towered house, with interesting displays on architecture in the Emirates. Hidden away directly behind Sheikh Saeed Al Maktoum House, the modest **Camel Museum** (Sat–Thur 8am–8pm, Fri 2–8pm; free) and Horse Museum (daily except Fri 8am–2pm; free) are of considerably less interest, although the exhibits on camel racing in the former – includ-

ing a creaking pair of anamatronic dromedaries – are worth a quick look.

*Heritage and Diving villages*
Further north, towards the mouth of the Creek, the **Heritage Village** ➒ (tel: 04 393 7151; Sat–Thur 8am–10.30pm, Fri 8–11am & 4.30–10.30pm; free) comprises a walled compound with traditional buildings arranged around a large sandy courtyard. It's usually fairly deserted during the day, but comes to life after dusk (particularly during the winter and local festivals) with souvenir shops, foodstalls (often run by local Emirati women) and occasional cultural performances. **The Diving Village** (same hours) next door is similar but smaller.

**Below:** the lanes of historic Bastakiya.

## BASTAKIYA

Retrace you steps back down the Creek and through Dubai Old Souk to the Dubai Museum (no hardship, given the cooling sea breezes and wonderful views). Just beyond the museum on your left you'll see the historic old **Bastakiya** quarter ➓, built in the early 1900s by merchants from Bastak in southern Iran (hence the name). This is the best-preserved traditional quarter in the city: a small but surprisingly disorientating labyrinth of narrow alleyways, flanked with tall, coral-and-limestone houses topped with dozens of wind towers. These were first introduced to Dubai by Iranian settlers, but have now become synonymous with the UAE.

### Food and Drink 🍴

**① BAIT AL WAKEEL**
Bur Dubai Old Souk tel: 04 353 0530; daily noon–10pm; $$
In the old Gray Mackenzie Building (*see p.28*), with seating either inside the attractively restored period interior or outside on the deck overlooking the Creek and a decent range of well-prepared mezze, plus a few Chinese options.

**② XVA GALLERY**
Bastakiya; tel: 04 353 5383; www.xvahotel.com; Sat–Thur 9am–7pm, Fri 10am–5pm; $$
Delightful courtyard café in a historic house that is now an art gallery and boutique hotel. The menu offers fresh and healthy vegetarian fare including salads, soups and sandwiches.

An early form of air conditioning, these square towers capture cool air and funnel it down into the houses below, while also allowing hot air to rise and escape.

The walls of each house were made of coral stone, which, thanks to its porous nature, has low thermal conductivity, keeping temperatures inside to a minimum. For privacy and security, there were no windows on the ground floor, just a few ventilation holes. Most of the houses are fairly plain from the outside but surprisingly ornate within, usually with spacious inner courtyards, shaded with trees and surrounded by arches and doorways. A number of heritage buildings have been opened as little museums (all free), giving you the chance to have a look inside, while others have been converted into small galleries and shops.

### Majlis Gallery

Right next to the entrance to the quarter, the **Majlis Gallery** ⑪ (tel: 04 353 6233, www.themajlisgallery.com; Sat–Thur 10am–6pm; free) is the oldest in the city, established in 1976 to showcase the work of UAE artists, as well as international ones with UAE ties. The gallery also sells traditional craft items, such as curved *khanjars* (traditional daggers worn by UAE nationals until the 1970s and still worn by men in neighbouring Oman), goatskin water bags and jewellery.

## Pearl Diving

Before 'black gold' there were pearls. In the centuries before oil was discovered, pearling was the mainstay of the Dubai economy, involving the majority of the male population. From June to September, boats of between 15 and 60 men stayed at sea for up to four months, moving from one pearl oyster bed to another and sheltering from storms on Gulf islets. Equipped with little more than a nose clip, ear plugs and finger pads, and surviving on a diet of fish and rationed water, the men would dive on weighted ropes to depths of around 15m (49ft) up to 50 times a day. In just two or three minutes underwater they could collect up to a dozen pearl oysters. Pearls were graded according to their size, colour and shape. In the early 20th century, the best pearls, or jiwan (a derivative of 'Grade One' or 'G-One'), could fetch 1,500 rupees, but while Dubai's pearl merchants grew wealthy, a diver's wages for the entire season could be as little as 30–60 rupees. Famous for their rose-colouring, Dubai pearls were traded in India, from where they were sent to Paris. The popularity of the Japanese cultured pearl from the 1930s devastated the Gulf industry, which struggled on for another decade until the last great pearling expedition sailed from Dubai in 1949.

### Coffee-Drinking

Traditional Arabian coffee (kahwa) is quite different from western coffee. It's made from green coffee beans and usually flavoured with cardamom and perhaps other herbs – very strong and slightly bitter. Poured from a distinctive pot, Arabian coffee is served in tiny cups without handles, which are refilled until the drinker 'wobbles' the cup from side to side, indicating that they have had enough – but remember that it's traditionally considered rude to take more than three cups.

**Above from left:** shisha pipes; a meeting at the XVA Gallery; a local Emirati man; *dhows* on the Creek.

## XVA Gallery

On the opposite side of Bastakiya, the **XVA Gallery** ⑫ (tel: 04 358 5117; www.xvagallery.com; Sun–Thur 11am–8pm, Sat noon–6pm; free) puts on shows of contemporary work from across the Middle East, and also has a lovely courtyard **coffee shop**, see ⑪②, plus atmospheric accommodation in traditional rooms *(see p.108)*.

## Sheikh Mohammed Centre

On the eastern side of Bastakiya, in yet another traditional building, the **Sheikh Mohammed Centre for Cultural Understanding** ⑬ (tel: 04 353 6666, www.cultures.ae; Sun–Thur 9am–6pm, Sat 9am–1pm; free except tours and lunch) was created to foster awareness and understanding of local Emirati culture – over 90 percent of Dubai's population are expa-

triates, and it's quite possible to spend long periods in the city without meeting a single UAE national. The centre is a non-profit-making organisation, established by and named after Dubai's ruler, which promotes mutual understanding among people from different cultures. Activities include walking tours of Bastakiya, guided tours of Jumeira Mosque *(see p.56)* and 'cultural lunches' during which you can meet local Emiratis over a traditional meal.

## SOUTHEAST OF BASTAKIYA

Southeast of Bastakiya, you can continue walking along beside the Creek – looking back, there are fine views of the clustered wind towers of Bastakiya and the tall white minaret of the mosque in the grounds of the

---

## A Dynamic Dynasty

Dubai's growth from the late 1950s to the present day is due mainly to Sheikh Rashid Bin Saeed Al Maktoum and his son Sheikh Mohammed. Sheikh Rashid, 'the Father of Dubai,' ruled from 1958 to 1990, building up the city's infrastructure to ensure that Dubai was well set up to exploit oil wealth when it finally came. When he died in 1990, his eldest son Sheikh Maktoum became ruler, but it was Sheikh Mohammed, younger son and Crown Prince, who was the new driving force behind the city's rapid development, leading the push towards a more diversified economy. Sheikh Maktoum died in 2006, and now 'Sheikh Mo' (as he is affectionately called, privately, by some of Dubai's residents), rules the emirate. Revered and respected by many Emiratis, he can occasionally be spotted driving around in his white Mercedes 4x4 with the number plate '1'.

---

## Food and Drink

**③ ANTIQUE BAZAAR**
Sheraton Four Points Bur Dubai, tel: 04 397 7444; Sat–Thur noon–3pm and 7pm–11pm, Fri 7–11pm; $$$
A ten-minute walk (or short taxi ride) inland from Bastakiya, this Indian restaurant looks like a room from a Rajasthani palace, backed up by a well-prepared range of North Indian meat and veg classics.

**④ KAN ZAMAN**
Creekside, Shindagha; tel: 04 393 9913; daily 6pm–1.30am; $
In a fine location near the mouth of the Creek, Kan Zaman has breezy outdoor and waterside seating and a good selection of Lebanese mezze, Turkish coffee and shisha pipes.

---

**Emiri Diwan**, or Ruler's Court. Continuing down the promenade you'll pass the large cemetery on your right which once marked the edge of the old town, while along the waterfront fishermen still wait for *sheirii*, *safi*, *neiser* and catfish to bite.

About 1km south of Bastakiya, past the British Embassy, a superb cluster of modern buildings can be seen rising up across the Creek. Particularly striking is the **National Bank of Dubai** ⑭ (1998), designed by Carlos Ott with a vast convex glass front shaped like a sail. The glassy façade reflects the water and the passing river traffic; it's particularly dramatic towards dusk, when it seems to be ablaze with the light of the setting sun.

To the right of the National Bank of Dubai stands the minimalist blue glass wedge of the **Dubai Chamber of Commerce** building. To the left stands the **Sheraton Hotel**, one of the oldest in Dubai, with its triangular façade, a bit like a ship's prow, jutting out into the water. Behind the Sheraton you'll notice the **Etisalat Tower**, the head-quarters for Dubai's first telecommunications company and instantly recognisable thanks to the enormous 'golf ball'-like structure on its roof.

Further right, **Al Maktoum Bridge** is one of three bridges that cross the Creek (the other two are in the Garhoud area) and, just visible behind that, the distinctive roof of the **Dubai Creek Golf & Yacht Club** *(see p.42)*. From here, it's a short taxi ride back to Khalid Bin Al Walid Road and the Four Points Sheraton hotel, where you'll find the **Antique Bazaar** (see ⑪③) restaurant, a fine spot for an evening meal. Alternatively, retrace your steps back along the Creek to **Kan Zaman** see ⑪④.

**Abra Commuters**
Around 15,000 commuters (mostly lower-paid workers) use these wooden water taxis to take them over the Creek every day. The boats were originally powered by oars, but now have rather more environmentally unfriendly diesel engines to propel them through the water.

**Below:** traditional hanging jars and dwelling at the Heritage Village, with a wind tower behind.

# DEIRA

*This leisurely day-long walking tour offers a rewarding wander around Deira's souks, while a couple of absorbing heritage buildings and a visit to the city's old wooden dhow anchorage round out the tour, before ending with cocktails at the Boardwalk.*

**Above from left:** Deira's waterfront; invitingly fresh produce at the Fruit and Vegetable Souk.

**DISTANCE** 6km (3.7 miles)
**TIME** A full day
**START** Gold Souk
**END** Dubai Creek Golf & Yacht Club
**POINTS TO NOTE**

To reach the starting point of the tour, either take a taxi directly to the Gold Souk or a taxi to Bur Dubai Abra Station and then an *abra* to Deira Old Souk Arbra Station, from where it's just a few minutes walk to the Gold Souk. At the very end of the tour you'll probably want to take a taxi from the southern *dhow* moorings to the Dubai Creek Golf & Yacht Club – this should cost around Dhs10.

**Below:** catch of the day at the Fish Souk.

The commercial heart of the old city, life in Deira still largely revolves around the souk. The shops may be largely modern, and jazzy neon signs may have replaced the traditional hand-painted boards, but business here is still conducted more or less as it has been for over a century past, with thousands of shoebox shops wedged into the district's rambling bazaars, retailing everything from cheap toys and textiles through to gold and frankincense – a far cry from the modern malls which dominate newer parts of Dubai. The district is also home to a number of other rewarding heritage sights, including the fine old Al Ahmadiya School and adjacent Heritage House, plus the memorable *dhow* moorings, with dozens of old-fashioned Arabian *dhows* tied up along the banks of the Creek.

The obvious place to begin any tour of Deira is at the **Gold Souk ❶** (most shops open Sat–Thur 10am–10pm, although some close in the afternoon from around 1–4pm, Fri 4–10pm), probably the most famous in Dubai, and certainly the most valuable. There are about a hundred shops here, lined up under a wooden roof, their windows overflowing with vast quantities of gold

jewellery ranging from florid Arabian designs through to more understated pieces – the traditional Emirati-style bracelets are particularly nice.

Gold here remains some of the most competitively priced in the world, attracting a colourful array of shoppers from West Africa, Russia, India and elsewhere. Jewellery is sold by weight (despite its intricacy, the quality of the workmanship isn't usually factored into the price). If you ask the price of an item, it will first be put on the scales and weighed, and its value calculated according to the day's gold price (which may be displayed in the shop). Asking for a 'small discount' or 'special price'

should help knock a further chunk off the price. At this point – and assuming you're still interested in buying the piece – it's time to start bargaining.

Many shops also sell silver and precious stones, while the area is also a major centre for Dubai's thriving trade in designer fakes – you'll not spend long in the souk without being approached with offers of 'cheap copy watch' or similar.

Walk out of the back (western) end of the Gold Souk, turn right onto Old Baladiya Street and follow it around onto Al Ahmadiya Street for a few minutes to reach Al Ahmadiya School and the Heritage House, a pair of neatly restored traditional

**Above:** men outside the Fish Souk.

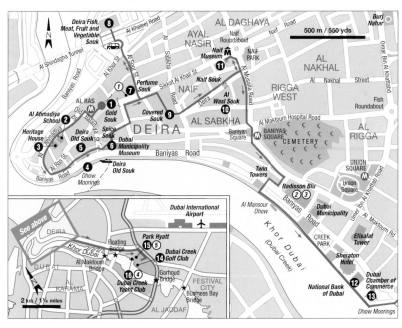

### Buying Gold
Dubai is one of the cheapest places in the world to buy gold. Jewellery is sold by weight, with the basic cost calculated according to the day's gold price (which might be posted inside the shop), although there's plenty of leeway for bargaining beyond this.

buildings now housing low-key museums and offering fascinating glimpses of life in old Dubai.

Established in 1912 by local pearl merchant Ahmad Bin Dalmouk (after whom it's named), **Al Ahmadiya School** ❷ (Al Ahmadiya Street; tel: 04 226 0286; 8am–7.30pm, Fri 2.30–7.30pm; free) was the first semi-formal school in Dubai. Pupils here were taught the Koran, Arabic calligraphy and arithmetic, while other subjects including history, literature and astronomy were subsequently added to the curriculum. Built in three phases, Al Ahmadiya School was initially a single-storey structure with 11 classrooms and a *liwan*, or veranda, around an inner courtyard, while the upper floor was added in 1920. In 1932, following the collapse of the pearl trade – and with it the local economy – the school was forced to close, but it reopened in 1937 with a government subsidy. In 1956, with the introduction of a formal education system for boys (1958 for girls), schools were expected to follow a regular curriculum that included English, sociology and more science subjects. Student numbers increased, and, by 1962, the school had 823 students – more than it could comfortably accommodate. In 1963, the school moved to a new, larger site, and the original building was closed.

### The building
By the mid 1990s, the building had become completely derelict and was in danger of collapsing completely until being meticulously restored by the Dubai Municipality's Historical Buildings Section using authentic building materials such as coral stone, gypsum and sandalwood. Like most of Dubai's traditional buildings, the

## Traditional Emirati houses

Traditional houses along the Gulf coast were built from locally available materials – usually pieces of coral stone bound together with pounded gypsum, with roofs made out of mangrove wood (or, in grander residences, Indian teak). The emphasis was on privacy and security: most houses have few windows and usually only one entrance. Inside, most dwellings were centred on large interior courtyards, providing space for children to play and livestock to graze. The majlis (meeting room) is another standard feature (plus, in larger establishments, a dedicated ladies' majlis as well).

Traditional houses were remarkably well adapted to their environment in the days before air-conditioning. The thick walls and smallness of windows both helped keep interiors cool, while wind towers captured any passing breezes and funnelled them down to the rooms below. Houses were also built close together, helping to create narrow and almost permanently shaded alleyways between.

### Bargaining
If you are interested in buying something at the Gold Souk, do not reveal your full interest to the seller. Start your offer low – at around half the amount you estimate you would finally like to spend.

decorative doorway opens into a courtyard, or *al housh*, surrounded by verandas and various rooms. The courtyard was the place where school assemblies were held and where pupils did their exercises and had their breaks.

The rooms around the courtyard now house some low-key exhibits covering the history of the school, including cute mannequins of pupils in traditional dress (and one rather scary-looking teacher). There are more classrooms upstairs, still equipped with their old wooden desks and chairs.

## HERITAGE HOUSE

Next to Al Ahmadiya School is the **Heritage House** ❸ (tel: 04 226 0216; Sat–Thur 8am–7.30pm; Fri 2.30–7.30pm; free). This was originally built in 1890 for Mohammed Bin Saeed Bin Muzaaina, but was subsequently acquired in 1910 by pearl trader Ahmad Bin Dalmouk, the pearl trader who expanded the house, as well as establishing the school next door. Like Al Ahmadiya School, the Heritage House was also restored in the mid-1990s and opened to the public in 2000 as a reminder of the city's pre-oil era.

Today, the 935 sq m (10,065 sq ft) building is preserved as it would have been in the 1940s and 1950s. This is one of best surviving examples of a traditional Emirati home, providing an atmospheric snapshot of the social life of Dubai's wealthier inhabitants during that period. Notable features include the separate men's and women's *majlis*, or meeting rooms, where guests would have sat on embroidered pillows around the edge of a Persian-carpet-

**Above from far left:** spectacular gold jewellery; Al Ahmadiya School.

**Souk opening hours**
There are no official opening hours in Deira's souks, although most shops usually open Sat–Thur 10am–1pm & 4pm–10pm, Fri 4–10pm; some shops in more touristy areas might also stay open throughout the afternoon.

**Below:** Heritage House interior.

**Above:** Burj Nahar; Deira mosque.

ed floor, drinking Arabic coffee and discussing the economic, social and political issues of the day.

### DHOW MOORINGS

Turn left out of the Heritage House and follow the road around to reach the Creek, then turn left again along the waterfront, until you reach Deira Old Souk Abra Station after a couple more minutes. Facing the Creek on your left is the warren of lanes and alleyways that make up Deira Old Souk (see below). Ahead of you, stretching down the waterfront, are the old city's **dhow moorings ❹**, with lines of traditional old wooden cargo boats moored up along the edge of the Creek – a unexpectedly old-fashioned sight amongst the modern traffic and office blocks.

Huge piles of cargo usually stand stacked up along the road here – anything from mounds of fizzy drinks to washing machines and the occasional car – waiting to be loaded up onto boats and shipped off overseas. Many of the *dhows* here head off to Iran (and many have Iranian crews), while some head further afield to India, Pakistan and East Africa. The impossibility of enforcing proper customs procedures along the crowded roadside has proved something of a headache for the authorities, given the relative ease with which boats here could be used to smuggle items in and out of the country, and attempts are being made to gradually move shipping to more secure facilities down the coast. For the time being, however, the *dhows* remain.

### DEIRA OLD SOUK

Turning away from the Creek, head into the attractive tangle of covered alleyways making up **Deira Old Souk ❺** (most shops open Sat–Thur 10am–10pm, although some close in the afternoon from around 1–4pm, Fri 4–10pm). Most of the souk's shops are now devoted to relatively mundane items like cheap toys, textiles and clothing. The most interesting part of the Old Souk is the **Spice Souk,** close to Deira Old Souk Abra Station. This is one of the prettiest corners of Deira, a few narrow alleyways with shops fronted by colourful sacks and trays of fragrant produce,

---

## Food and Drink  🍴

**① ASHWAQ**
Sikkat Al Khail Road, near the entrance to the Gold Souk; daily 10am–10pm; $
A popular little café, serving up juicy shawarma sandwiches and big cups of various fruit juices – get your lunch then grab a seat at one of the pavement tables for some classic Deira people-watching.

**② LA MODA**
Radisson SAS Hotel Dubai Deira Creek, Baniyas Road; tel: 04 205 7444; www.deiracreek.dubai.radissonsas.com; lunch 12.30–3pm; $$$
This is a stylish contemporary Italian restaurant offering a good selection of dishes. The seafood risotto is a favourite.

**③ YUM!**
Radisson Blu tel: 04 222 7171, www.deiracreek. dubai.radissonsas.com; daily noon–11.30pm; $$
Attractive modern noodle bar with brisk service and flavoursome pan-Asian dishes – mainly Thai, plus a few Chinese, Malay, Indonesian and Singaporean dishes.

---

although unfortunately it's also shrinking due to competition from local hypermarkets like the Carrefour, which is where most modern Dubaians now go for their spices. Goods on offer include mainstream spices (plus relatively inexpensive saffron) and other local cooking ingredients like dried cucumbers and lemons, as well as piles of rose petals, used to scent tea. The souk is also a good place to buy frankincense, sold in various different forms and grades, including cheaper, reddish Somali frankincense and more expensive Omani grades; frankincense burners can also be bought in the souk for a few dirhams. Most stalls also sell natural cosmetic products such as pumice and *alum*, a clear rock crystal used as a kind of mineral aftershave.

Right in front of the Spice Souk (opposite Deira Old Souk Abra Station) stands the small **Dubai Municipality Museum** ❻ (tel: 04 345 3636; Sat–Thur 7.30am–3pm; free), occupying the former headquarters of the Dubai Municipality – a simple but elegant, two-storey structure with a long wooden balcony offering fine views over the commercial hustle and bustle below. Inside, the museum hosts a modern array of civic documents and old photographs.

## PERFUME SOUK

From here, you're almost back to the Gold Souk, and the start of the walk. Returning to the Gold Souk entrance, head east for a block along Sikkat Al Khail Street and then turn left up Al Soor Street. Dozens of traditional perfume shops line these two streets hereabouts, an area commonly known as the **Perfume Souk** ❼ (most shops open Sat–Thur 10am–10pm, although some close in the afternoon from around 1–4pm, Fri 4–10pm). Shops stock a mix of western brands (not necessarily genuine) and more flowery local scents. Many places can also mix up a bespoke perfume for you on request from the rows of glass scent bottles lined up behind the counters.

## FISH, MEAT AND VEG SOUK

Continue to the top of Al Soor Street and across the Gold Souk Bus Station on the far side of which a footbridge crosses the busy Al Khaleej Road to

**Above from far left:** traditional dancers in Creek Park; cargo *dhows* moored on the Deira quayside.

**Below:** a fisherman repairing his nets.

Above from left:
defensive tower at
Deira's Naif Museum;
colourful fabric; logo
in the pool at Dubai
Creek Golf & Yacht
Club.

## A Developing District

Together with Bur
Dubai, Deira formed
the commercial heart
of old Dubai, but it
was also the district
where new services
emerged: the children
of Shindagha and Bur
Dubai crossed to
Deira for an
education, after the
city's first school was
established here in
1912, and people
came to Deira for
medical treatment
after the first hospital
on the Trucial Coast,
Al Maktoum Hospital,
was established here
in 1949.

reach the **Fish, Meat and Veg Souk** , the old city's main wholesale area for all things edible. Before venturing inside, take time to wander among the ice lorries parked to the right of the main building. The fish are kept here in iceboxes and either wheeled into the market by porters or sold to bulk buyers such as restaurateurs. You'll be amazed at the variety of shapes and sizes of fish, and, here in the sun, you can also appreciate their often stunning colours. Red snappers, belt fish, kingfish – up to 1.5m (5-ft) -long – sardines and baby sharks are among those weighed and tossed into barrows or flat-bed trucks. In the market proper, walk between the trays of fish towards the sound of chopping at the top left of the hall. Here, buyers can have their fish descaled, filleted and diced by an army of knife-wielding workers in blue overalls.

Next to the fish souk – but definitely not for those of a squeamish disposition – is the smaller **Meat Souk**, where skinned goats (the carcasses come complete with tails), lambs (without tails)

and cows hang. Somewhat easier on both the nose and the eye is the **Fruit and Vegetable Souk** in the next hall, a particularly good place to buy a wide range of dates from across the Gulf.

Assuming the sight of all this food has made you hungry, return down Al Soor Street for a classic Dubai lunch of shwarma at the small but enduringly popular **Ashwaq** (see ⑪①), a no-frills little café which serves up more-ish shawarmas and big fruit juices, while the pavement tables are one of the best places in Deira to people-watch.

### THE COVERED SOUK AND AL WASL SOUK

Continue east down Sikkat Al Khail Road back past the junction with Al Soor St and then dive right down any of the various little lanes to reach the **Covered Souk** ❾ (most shops open Sat–Thur 10am–10pm, although some close in the afternoon from around 1–4pm, Fri 4–10pm). The shops and merchandise here are fairly humdrum compared to other souks in Deira – household items, cheap toys and clothes predominate – although it's an enjoyable area for an aimless and disorientating wander, attempting to pick a route between the shops and piles of merchandise through the labyrinth of tiny lanes and alleyways.

Keep heading east and, all being well, you'll come out somewhere along Al Sabkha Road. Cross this and continue through **Al Wasl Souk** ❿ – even bigger and more disorientating, particular-

Food and Drink 🍴

④ THE BOARDWALK
Dubai Creek Golf & Yacht Club, near Deira City Centre; tel:
04 295 6000; www.dubaigolf.com; Sun–Thur noon–midnight,
Fri and Sat 8am–midnight; $$
The menu of international food is reliable enough, but it's the
terrific Creek and city views from the outdoor seating on the
restaurant's eponymous boardwalk that really steal the show.

⑤ THE TERRACE PARK HYATT HOTEL
Park Hyatt Hotel; tel: 04 317 2222; dubai.park.hyatt.com; $$$
A very smooth Creekside cocktail bar, with a superior (if pricey)
drinks list, discreet ambient music and wonderful waterside views.

ly after dark, when the pavements are thronged with crowds of local shoppers. There are all sorts of different routes through the bazaar, although it's more fun to wander where the urge takes you, aiming ultimately to come out around the northeastern corner of the souk somewhere near the junction of Sikkat Al Khail Street and Al Musalla Road.

## NAIF MUSEUM

At the far eastern end of Sikkat Al Khail Street, close to the junction with All Musalla Road, stands the interesting but little-visited **Naif Museum** ⓫ (tel: 04 227 6484; Sat–Thur 8am–2pm; free) in **Naif Fort**, the first headquarters of Dubai Police, when the force was established by Sheikh Rashid in 1956.

The fort, which remains a police station today, was added to a single square defensive tower constructed in 1939 to bolster the defence of the northern approach to Dubai. The original tower – made of coral stone, shells and gypsum – still stands, while the rest of the fort was reconstructed in 1994 on the orders of Sheikh Mohammed (himself a former head of Dubai Police and Public Security in 1968, a position to which he was appointed at the age of just 19).

The museum is housed in a room below the tower. Among the exhibits are early handguns and rifles, a stock restraint, known as Al Hataba, for prisoners' feet, and uniforms, including the current military-style

green outfit and the first police *kandoura*, which was white with a red belt and red epaulettes.

## SOUTH ALONG THE CREEK

From the Naif Museum it's a ten-minute walk down busy All Musalla Road to Baniyas Square, at the centre of modern Deira, and then onto the Creek. A wide and attractive waterfront walkway heads south from here, running past the Radisson Blu hotel (formerly the InterContinental, the city's first five-star when it opened in 1970) and a line of tourist *dhows* moored up along the waterfront. The Radisson Blu has a number of good venues for a late lunch or early dinner, including **La Moda** and **Yum!** (see ⓫② and ③).There are fine views back up the Creek towards the city centre from here, with the wind towers of Bastakiya *(see p.30)* over the water, framed by the minarets of the Juma Grand Mosque and Emiri Diwan Mosque.

**Below:** textile merchant at Naif Souk.

**Above:** the iconic sails of the Golf & Yacht Club.

**Building Houses**
Early dwellings in Deira were made of palm fronds, but after fire ravaged the community in 1894 more substantial homes were constructed, using coral stone and gypsum. By 1908, according to the historian and geographer G.G. Lorimer, there were 1,600 houses and 350 shops in Deira, compared to just 200 houses and 50 shops in Bur Dubai.

**Below:** Dubai Creek Golf & Yacht Club.

A leisurely 10-minute stroll brings you to the cluster of modernist Creekside buildings which you may already have seen from the Bur Dubai side of the water *(see p.33)*, including the landmark **National Bank of Dubai building** ⑫ and the triangular-topped **Dubai Chamber of Commerce** ⑬, as well as the Sheraton Hotel, and the Etisalat Tower, surmounted by its distinctive 'golf ball'.

Immediately south of the Dubai Chamber of Commerce, a second set of *dhow* moorings line the banks of the Creek, usually home to dozens more traditional wooden *dhows*, surreally framed by the glass-fronted modernist buildings behind.

## THE GOLF & YACHT CLUB

The southern end of the *dhow* moorings is marked by Maktoum Bridge, the first in the city when it was opened in 1963. Beyond here stretches the district of Garhoud and the expansive grounds of the beautiful **Dubai Creek**

**Golf Club** ⑭ (although it's not much fun walking down the busy Baniyas Road, so get a cab – around Dhs10).

The club is best known for its famous clubhouse, an eye-catching structure inspired by the triangular sails of the traditional Arabian *dhow* and looking a bit like a Dubai version of the Sydney Opera House in miniature. Close by stands the idyllic **Park Hyatt** hotel ⑮, with its pretty, rather Moorish-looking swathe of white-walled, blue-domed buildings overlooking the adjacent **Dubai Creek Yacht Club** ⑯ where dozens of expensive yachts sit moored up alongside the Creek. This is also where you'll find the lively **Boardwalk** restaurant (see ⑪④).

There's a surprisingly good range of places to eat and drink here, either in the golf clubhouse, at the yacht club or in the Park Hyatt. The **Terrace** bar at the Park Hyatt (see ⑪⑤) is particularly lovely, with sublime Creekside views past the yachts and down to the high-rises of Deira and Sheikh Zayed Road.

# OUD METHA, KARAMA AND SATWA

*This tour threads its way through the necklace of suburbs dividing the old city centre from the more upmarket, high-rise districts further south – a part of the Dubai often missed by visitors, although there are numerous attractions tucked away here amidst the concrete sprawl.*

In contrast to the newer suburbs of Jumeirah Beach Residence and Downtown Dubai, this part of the city is less pristine, with a charmingly rugged edge that is a welcome break from the immaculately designed expat havens. Explore Oud Metha, before continuing to bustling Karama and Satwa, two of the city's oldest and most personable working-class districts.

## OUD METHA

South of Bur Dubai, the district of **Oud Metha** is something of a hotchpotch – somewhat lacking in character or streetlife, but home to some of the inner-city's biggest tourist developments, including the spectacular Wafi complex and the adjacent Raffles hotel and Khan Murjan souk.

### Creekside Park

Stretching south of Maktoum Bridge, the spacious **Creekside Park ①** (daily 8am–11pm, Thur–Sat until 11.30pm; Dhs5) offers one of the few sizeable open areas in the congested city centre. It's a pleasant place for a stroll, with fine views over the Creek to the quaint buildings of the Park Hyatt hotel and distinctive Dubai Creek Golf Club on the far side of the water. Even finer views can be had from the park's rickety old cable car (Dhs25, children Dhs15).

---

**DISTANCE** 9km (5.5 miles)
**TIME** A full day
**START** Creekside Park, Oud Metha
**END** Al Diyafah Street, Satwa
**POINTS TO NOTE**

Take a taxi to Creekside Park, and then catch a cab or continue on foot to Wafi. From here, catch another cab for the short journey to Karama souk, followed by a third cab from Karama for the quick ride across to Satwa. If you start the tour around midday, you can aim to have a late lunch either in Wafi or adjacent Khan Murjan and then continue over to Karama towards dusk before heading over to Satwa for an evening meal and a chance to sample the after-dark streetlife of one of Dubai's most vibrant areas.

---

**Above:**
Creekside Park.

**Kidding Around**
Further entertainment for children in the Oud Metha area can be found at the Wonderland complex, at the southern end of Creekside Park, next to Garhoud Bridge (daily 10am–10pm; adults Dhs15, children aged 4–12 Dhs10; tel: 04 324 1222; www.wonderland uae.com). This rather old-fashioned theme park is packed with a variety of rides (mostly Dhs5–10 each) and other attractions including a rollercoaster, powercarts, pirate ship, western trains, soft-play area, bumper cars, a horror house and the modest Splashland water park (daily 10am–6pm).

## Bedouin Camels

Historically, not only were camels used for getting around, but their milk and meat would provide valuable protein for an entire Bedu family for months on end. Camel hide was used to make bags and utensils, and the hair was woven into fine outer garments for men, known as *bisht*.

### Children's City

The park is also home to the excellent **Children's City** ❷ (tel: 04 334 0808; www.childrencity.ae; Sat–Thur 9am–8pm, Fri 3–9pm; Dhs15, children 3–15 years Dhs10; children under two, free; family ticket for two adults and two children Dhs40). If you've got kids in tow, this is a rewarding destination, with a fun, interactive range of galleries exploring various themes including science, nature, space exploration and cultures of the world. Even without kids, it's worth a peek at the City's striking buildings, painted in bright primary colours and looking a bit like some kind of supersized Lego construction.

### Dubai Dolphinarium

Just outside the park, next to Gate #1, the **Dubai Dolphinarium** ❸ (tel: 04 336 9773, www.dubaidolphinarium. ae, adults Dhs100, children Dhs50) offers another fun destination for kids. The Dolphinarium stages daily shows (Mon–Sat at 11am & 6pm, also Fri & Sat at 3pm) featuring the centre's three bottlenose dolphins and four seals, with the obligatory jumping through hoops and flipping of balls. A more rewarding (and expensive) alternative is to go for a swim with the dolphins (Dhs400 for a group session; reservations required).

### Wafi

Exit Creekside Park via Gate #1, then turn left down Riyadh Road and then right down 26th Street, around the back of the huge Grand Hyatt hotel, the largest in the city until the opening of Atlantis The Palm *(see p.63)* in 2008. Turn right down Street 26 and you will reach the glitzy **Wafi** ❹ complex (www.waficity.com; daily 10am–10pm, Thur & Fri until midnight). The centrepiece of Oud Metha, Wafi looks like a little slice of Las Vegas dropped into the middle of the Gulf, with a comic-book, Egyptian-style design featuring a zany mishmash of huge pharaonic statues, heiroglyphs, spectacular

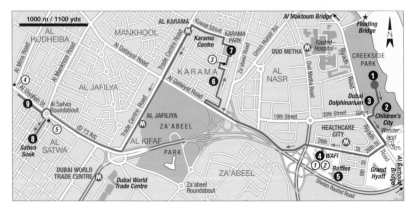

stained-glass windows and half a dozen miniature pyramids dotted across the sprawling rooflines. It's cheesy but entertaining, while the complex also provides one of the city's most attractive shopping and eating destinations – **Elements** café (see ⑪①) is a particularly appealing spot for a light lunch or drink.

### Khan Murjan

Beneath the Wafi complex is the beautiful **Khan Murjan** souk (www. wafi.com; daily 10am–10pm, Thur and Fri until midnight), inspired by the legendary 14th-century Khan Murjan souk in Baghdad. This is one of Dubai's finest exercises in Orientalist kitsch, with virtually every available surface covered in lavishly detailed Arabian-style design featuring elaborate Moroccan-style tilework, intricately carved wooden doors and ceilings, and huge hanging lamps. The souk is home to over a hundred shops

## Food and Drink

#### ① ELEMENTS
Wafi, Oud Metha; daily 10am–midnight; $$
Funky little place in the Wafi complex serving up a wide selection of reasonably priced café fare ranging from sandwiches, salads and pizzas through to dim sum and sushi, plus more substantial meat and fish mains.

#### ② KHAN MURJAN RESTAURANT
Khan Murjan Souk, Oud Metha; daily 10am–11.30pm; $$$
Beautiful courtyard restaurant at the heart of Khan Murjan Souk. The menu features an unusually wide range of Middle Eastern dishes, from mainstream Lebanese grills and mezze through to traditional Gulf dishes like fouga and goboli.

#### ③ KARACHI DURBAR
Karama, between Karama Souk and Karama Park; daily 10am–10pm; $
A long-established curry house dishing up huge portions of tasty Pakistani-style chicken or mutton curries at bargain-basement prices.

#### ④ AL MALLAH
Al Diyafah St, Satwa; daily 10am–10pm; $
One of several good Lebanese cafés along Al Diyafah Street, with a good range of inexpensive Middle Eastern mezze, snacks and meals (including good grills and shwarma) and plenty of seating on the pavement outside – a great place to watch the nightlife of Satwa roll past.

#### ⑤ RAVI'S
Just off Satwa Roundabout, Satwa; daily 10am–11pm; $
This legendary little café remains enduringly popular with locals, expats and tourists alike for its cheap and tasty Pakistani-style chicken, mutton and vegetable curries, while the outdoor seating offers a good (if noisy) perch from which to enjoy the passing streetlife.

retailing all manner of upmarket Arabian (plus some Indian) handicrafts, while the superb **Khan Murjan Restaurant** (see ①②) at the heart of the souk offers a memorable venue for lunch.

### Raffles

Next door to Wafi – and continuing the Egyptian theme – the vast postmodern pyramid of **Raffles hotel** ❺ (www.raffles.com) provides Oud Metha with its most dramatic landmark, visible for miles around and particularly impressive after dusk, when the glass-walled summit of the pyramid is lit up from within, glowing magically in the darkness. Inside, the main foyer is well worth a look, with huge Egyptian-style columns covered in lavish heiroglyph. It's also worth a visit, later in the evening for a drink in the New Asia Bar at the very top of the pyramid, with stylish contemporary décor and sweeping city views.

From Wafi, it's a short taxi ride (around Dhs10) north to Karama Souk – it is easy to find a taxi, you'll find several lined up outside the main entrance to Wafi.

### KARAMA

**Karama** ❻ is a hive of activity; the area is home to many of the lower-paid expats, predominately from India and the Philippines who largely provide the city with its taxi drivers, waitresses, housemaids and construction workers. The area offes a refreshingly different insight into life in the city away from the tourist fleshpots and sky-age architecture.

### Karama Souk

This district is centred on the busy **Karama Souk** (most shops open Sat–Thur 10am–10pm, although some close in the afternoon from around 1–4pm, Fri 4–10pm), basically a pair of open-air concrete arcades stuffed with dozens of Indian-run shops selling all manner of clothes, shoes, DVDs and household items, plus a decent range of souvenirs. The souk is best known as the epicentre for Dubai's roaring trade in designer fakes – imitation bags, watches, sunglasses and other counterfeit-branded items, as well as pirated DVDs – although following government crackdowns these are occasionally kept out of sight in backrooms behind the various shops. You won't get more than a few paces into the souk before being regaled with offers of 'cheap copy watches' and the like. The quality of many of the fakes is surprisingly high, although prices can be unexpectedly steep – if you do decide to buy, check workmanship carefully and bargain like mad.

### Karama Park and Kuwait Street

Immediately north of the souk lies **Karama Park** ❼, a pleasant square of grass surrounded by dozens of inexpensive but generally excellent curry houses, such as the **Karachi Durbar** (see ①③). This is the social heart of the suburb, usually with half a dozen games of cricket in progress after dark, and crowds of strolling residents.

Turn west (left) at the end of the park to reach Kuwait Street, Karama's main thoroughfare, where you'll find the modest Karama Centre, home to some interesting little shops selling a colourful selection of richly embroidered saris and shalwar kameez. The whole strip is particularly lively after dark.

## SATWA

From Kuwait Street, catch a taxi for the short ride (roughly Dhs10) to the Satwa Roundabout, at the heart of the neighbouring suburb of Satwa. South of the roundabout is **Satwa Souk ⓫**, a hub for the district's Indian community, with an engaging string of low-key shops and a forest of neon signs.

Retrace your steps to Satwa Roundabout and then head west along **Al Diyafah Street ⓬**, Satwa's de facto high street. This is one of the most pleasant places in the city to explore after dark, with broad, tree-lined pavements dotted with a long string of cafés and restaurants, including several excellent Lebanese cafés. The unpretentious strip attracts a refreshingly mixed crowd of Dubai's multicultural population and locals, expats and tourists come here to stroll, people watch from the many pavement cafés and converse – this is Dubai on a refreshingly human scale. For food, good Lebanese mezze and shawarma can be found at **Al Mallah** (see ⓘ④) on Al Diyafah Street, while close by, just off Satwa Roundabout, is the ever-popular **Ravi's** (see ⓘ⑤).

# 4

# SHEIKH ZAYED ROAD AND DOWNTOWN DUBAI

*The futuristic Sheikh Zayed Road and Downtown Dubai development show Dubai at its most brazenly futuristic and wildly ambitious, with a long string of neck-straining skyscrapers leading south towards the cloud-capped Burj Khalifa, the world's tallest building.*

**DISTANCE** 5km (3.1 miles)
**TIME** A full day
**START** Dubai World Trade Centre
**END** Downtown Dubai
**POINTS TO NOTE**

Exactly how long this tour lasts depends largely on how much time you plan on spending in the Dubai Mall, either shopping or exploring the its other leisure activities – you could get through the tour in a brisk half-day, although just as easily (and perhaps more enjoyably) spend twice as long. Start by taking the metro to the World Trade Centre metro station, or alternatively catching a cab. Make sure that you're in Downtown Dubai after nightfall, when the magnificent Dubai Fountain springs into life.

**Below:** Emirates Tower interior

Record-breaking developments are seldom far away in this part of town, including not only the world's tallest building, but also its biggest shopping mall, largest fountain and tallest hotel. If you're looking for traditional Arabia, you've come to the wrong place. If you want extravagant sci-fi architecture and postmodern urban pizzazz, however, few other places on the planet can match this part of Dubai.

This day-long tour starts at the landmark World Trade Centre before heading south between the massed skyscrapers of Sheikh Zayed Road and then onto Downtown Dubai and the Burj Khalifa.

## SHEIKH ZAYED ROAD

**Sheikh Zayed Road** is one of Dubai's iconic images: a huge, twelve-lane highway flanked on either side by rows of densely packed skyscrapers, whose towering façades create an almost unbroken wall of glass and metal, like some kind of architectural canyon. The road itself is one of the busiest in the city, part of the main highway between Dubai and Abu Dhabi (and named after the famous ruler of the latter), while

the city's futuristic metro, with its distinctive pod-shaped stations, also runs down the road, offering fine views from its elevated track.

## Dubai World Trade Centre

At the northern end of Sheikh Zayed Road, next to Za'abeel Roundabout, stands the **Dubai World Trade Centre** ❶. Easily overlooked, this relatively modest, decidedly old-fashioned construction was actually the first high-rise in Dubai when it opened in 1979, and one of the first buildings of any kind in the Sheikh Zayed Road area, which was then largely desert. The building was widely considered an enormous white elephant at the time, but proved remarkably successful, kick-starting development in the south of the city.

From the Trade Centre it's a 10-minute walk south to the Emirates Towers. Dubai's sprawling International Convention and Exhibition Centre lies away to your left, while to your right, on the far side of the road, is the distinctive **Fairmont Hotel** ❷, designed to resemble an enormous postmodern wind tower.

## Emirates Towers

Standing proud above the northern end of Sheikh Zayed, the twin **Emirates Towers** ❸ were the tallest in the city upon completion in 2000 (the taller tower was also the highest in the Middle East at 355m (1,165ft)). They've since been outstripped locally by both the Almas Tower in Dubai Marina and, most notably, by the gargantuan Burj Khalifa (see p.53) just

down the road, but remain two of the most distinctive, and most beautiful, modern buildings in the city, with their unusual triangular summits and huge glass and aluminium façades which appear to glow in the fierce desert light.

The larger of the two towers (off limits to the general public) houses the headquarters of Emirates airlines and the principal offices of Dubai's ruler Sheikh Mohammad and his inner circle. The smaller tower has been taken over to the upmarket

**Above from far left:**
High-rise buildings along Sheikh Zayed Road; Dubai World Trade Centre; Emirates Towers.

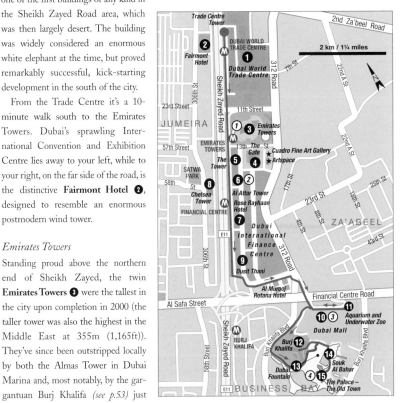

Jumeirah Emirates Towers, the leading business hotel in the city – well worth a look for the spectacular atrium, with glass-sided elevators shuttling up and down overhead or, even better, for a drink or meal at **Vu's Restaurant or Bar** *(see p.117 and p.121)* close to the summit of the building, with peerless views over the city below. For lunch, **The Noodle House** (see ⑨①), in the upmarket Boulevard shopping mall beneath the towers, is an excellent spot for a brisk and tasty bite.

### Dubai International Financial Centre

Immediately south of the Emirates Towers stretches the **Dubai International Financial Centre**

**(DIFC)**. The main landmark here is **The Gate** building ❹, an unusual structure resembling an office block-cum-archway, with a spacious courtyard in its centre. The building is home to the Dubai Stock Exchange, while the adjacent Gate Village Complex is home to a number of upmarket art galleries (see below).

### Art galleries at the DIFC

The DIFC complex provides a rather unlikely home to a surprisingly good range of galleries, serving as one of the leading hubs of the city's burgeoning visual arts scene. Top venues include Artspace (The Gate Village, Building no.3, Podium Level; tel: 04 323 0820, www.artspace-dubai.com), dedicat-

**Below:** a grocery store with the Emirates Towers in the background.

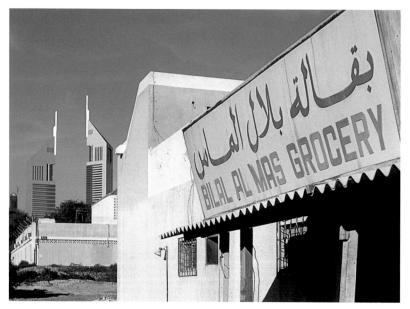

ed to contemporary Middle Eastern painters and sculptures; and Cuadro Fine Art Gallery (Gate Village, Building no.10; tel: 04 425 0400, www.cuadroart.com), which has a slightly more international flavour, although again with a strong Middle East emphasis, and a branch of **XVA Gallery** (see p.30).

*South along Sheikh Zayed Road*

Continuing south along Sheikh Zayed Road, either in a cab or peering out of the Dubai Metro, you will see that the highway is hemmed in either side by a long string of elongated skyscrapers packed in side by side. The buildings here offer a comprehensive compendium of Dubai's archetypal modern design, ranging from the functional through to the quirky and the downright bizarre.

Notable buildings along the east side of the road include **The Tower ❺**, an attractive structure topped with a pyramidal summit; the **Al Attar Tower ❻**, its plain plate-glass walls edged with enormous golden discs; and the elegant **Rose Rayhaan** hotel ❼ (the tallest hotel in the world, at 333m (1,093ft), having taken the record off the nearby Burj Al Arab), a soaring, pencil thin edifice topped with a small globe which lights up at night. Opposite the Rose Rayhaan, on the west side of the road, stands the massive **Chelsea Tower ❽**, its summit adorned with what looks like an enormous toothpick. Further south, at the end of the strip, is perhaps the most distinctive building of them all, the **Dusit Thani** hotel ❾, a bow-legged

colossus inspired by the shape of the traditional Thai *wai*, a prayer-like gesture of welcome. **The Shakespeare & Co.** café (see ⑪②), is a great place for a drink or light lunch.

## DOWNTOWN DUBAI

Continuing past the Dusit Thani hotel, turn left down the side road which winds around past the Al Murooj Rotana hotel and brings you out, after about a five minute walk, on to Financial Centre Road, opposite the main entrance to The Dubai Mall. This is part of the massive Downtown Dubai development opened in 2010 and built at an estimated cost of a cool $20 billion. The development features a string of attractions which, in true Dubai style, all have record-breaking claims, including The Dubai Mall itself (apparently the world's largest), along with the world's biggest fountain and, most notably, its tallest building, the sky-high Burj Khalifa.

**Above from left:**
The Gold Souk at The Dubai Mall; Dubai's dramatic skyline; The Burj Khalifa behind The Dubai Mall.

**Streets Ahead**
Sheikh Zayed Road is one of the best places in Dubai to appreciate the city's futuristic Dubai Metro, which arrows down the strip along an elevated track, dotted with eye-catching stations resembling enormous metallic pods. The ride down the road on the Metro is also well worth taking for its bird's-eye views of the streets and suburbs below - and the glass high-rises either side.

### The Dubai Mall

Shopping opportunities don't come much bigger than the gargantuan **The Dubai Mall** ❿ (daily 10am–10pm, Thur–Sat until midnight; www.thedubaimall.com). The entire complex covers a total area of 12 million square feet, with over 1,200 shops spread across four floors, making it impressively vast and a fantastic retail experience, even if the sheer size of the place can make a shopping trip here feel a bit like a long-distance hike.

Flagship outlets include branches of the famous Galleries Lafayette and Bloomingdales department stores, a huge branch of the Japanese bookseller Kinokuniya and an offshoot of London's famous Hamleys toy store. There's also a vast selection of upmar-

ket designer stores, mainly concentrated along 'Fashion Avenue', complete with its own catwalk, an Armani café, and a stunning Gold Souk decorated in an attractive Arabian design.

Shops apart, the mall also boasts a host of other leisure attractions. Children will enjoy the state-of-the-art **SEGA Republic** theme park and **KidZania** educational play area which allows kids to role play in a city created just for them, while there's also an Olympic-size ice rink and the Dubai Aquarium and Underwater Zoo *(see opposite)*. The mall is also home to well over a hundred cafés and restaurants, many of them located either along the waterside terrace at the back of the mall overlooking the Dubai Fountain, or along The Grove, an attractive 'out-

**Above:** children enthralled by the sights at the Dubai Aquarium.

## Food and Drink

### ② SHAKESPEARE & CO
Al Attar Business Tower, 37 Street, Sheikh Zayed Road; daily 10am–10pm; $$
A chintzy European-style café tucked away halfway down Sheikh Zayed Road and a nice place for a coffee or light lunch. The menu includes soups, salads, sandwiches and crepes along with substantial mains.

### ③ ORGANIC FOODS & CAFÉ
Dubai Mall; Sun–Wed 10am–10pm, Thur–Sat until midnight; $$
Part of the mall's basement strip of food outlets, this organic food store, has a homely café serving up wholesome dishes including soups, sandwiches and salads, plus international mains ranging from burgers, fish and chips and pasta through to steaks and stir fries. A peaceful spot compared to the other eateries in the mall.

### ④ THIPTARA
The Palace Hotel, Old Town, Downtown Dubai; tel: 04-428 7961; daily 7pm–midnight; $$$$
If you fancy pushing the boat out in Downtown Dubai, this beautiful Thai restaurant is the place to head for. Set in a traditional wooden pavilion jutting out into the waters of the lake behind the Dubai Mall, it offers peerless views of the Burj Khalifa and Dubai Fountain. The menu concentrates on sumptuous Bangkok-style seafood, plus meat and a few veg options.

door' streetscape under a retractable roof. If you fancy something to eat, the **Organic Foods** café (see 🍴③, *p.51*) in the basement offers good and inexpensive food.

## Dubai Aquarium

Just inside the mall's main entrance lies the **Dubai Aquarium and Underwater Zoo ⓫** (www.thedubaiaquarium.com; Sun–Wed 10am–10pm, Thur–Sat 10am–midnight; Dhs50, including the underwater viewing tunnel). Towering over the surrounding shops is the aquarium's spectacular 'viewing panel': a huge, floor-to-ceiling transparent acrylic panel filled with an extraordinary array of marine life, ranging from sand-tiger sharks and stingrays, through to colourful shoals of tiny tropical fish. You can ride a glass-bottom boat (Dhs25) across the top of the tank, walk through the underwater tunnel (Dhs25, children Dhs20) which leads through the middle, or even go 'diving with the sharks' (advance bookings required).

The Underwater Zoo upstairs is more likely to appeal to children than to adults, with displays themed on various types of marine habitat and featuring an array of wildlife ranging from tiny cichlids and poison-dart frogs through to otters, penguins and seals.

## Burj Khalifa

Walk across the mall and go out through the rear exit from the lower-ground (LG) floor from the Star Atrium. Ahead of you stretches the large lake (where the **Dubai Fountain** is located, *see p.54*) and a small footbridge leading to **Old Town** *(see p.55)*.

To begin with, however, you'll probably only have eyes for the staggering **Burj Khalifa ⓬**, the world's tallest building, rising up on your right. Opened in early 2010, the Burj Khalifa (828m /2,716ft) has obliterated all previous records for the world's tallest man-made structures, smashing the record for the world's tallest building (formerly held by Taipei 101 in Taiwan, at 509m) by a staggering 300m. The tower also holds claim to a host of other superlatives, including the building with the most floors (160), the world's highest and fastest elevators, plus highest mosque (158th floor) and swimming pool (76th floor).

The Burj was designed by Adrian Smith of the Chicago architectural firm Skidmore, Owings and Merrill (whose other high-rise creations include the Willis Tower, formerly the Sears Tower, in Chicago, and New York's 1 World Trade Center). The simple but elegant design is based on an unusual Y-shaped ground plan, where three projecting wings are gradually stepped back as the tower rises, so that the entire building becomes progressively narrower as it gains height.

The astonishing size of the Burj Khalifa and distinctively tapering outline is hard to grasp close up – the whole thing is best appreciated from a distance, from where you can properly grasp its jaw-dropping size, and the degree to which it dwarfs the surrounding highrises, many of which are considerable structures in their own right.

**Above from far left:** the Dubai Aquarium; the Burj Khalifa.

**The Burj**
The Burj Khalifa was originally known as the Burj Dubai. The unexpected name change was announced during the launch party as a gesture of gratitude towards Abu Dhabi's ruler, Sheikh Khalifa Bin Zayed Al Nahyan, for crucial financial assistance during the credit crunch.

### Visiting The Burj Khalifa

Much of the tower is occupied by around 900 very exclusive residential apartments, while 15 of the lower floors are given over to the world's first Armani hotel (www.armanihotels.com). The easiest way to visit the tower is to take the expensive trip to 'At the Top', the misleadingly named observation deck (on floor 124 – there are actually 160 floors in total). Tours leave from the ticket counter on the lower-ground floor of the The Dubai Mall. Tickets cost Dhs100 if pre-booked online at www.burjkhalifa.ae or pre-purchased at the ticket counter. If you want to go up without a prior reserva-

tion, you'll have to fork out a mighty Dhs400. Make sure you book well in advance – there's usually a waiting list of a good week to go up the tower.

### Dubai Fountain

Lying between the Burj Khalifa and the Dubai Mall is a large lake, surrounded by attractive pedestrianised waterfront promenades. Inserted into the section of the lake closest to The Dubai Mall is the spectacular **Dubai Fountain** ⓭. Standing in the shadow of the world's tallest building, this is, appropriately enough, purported to be the world's largest fountain at 275m (900ft) long, illuminated with over

**Below:** Burj Khalifa.

6,000 lights and with water-canons capable of shooting jets of water up to 150m (490ft) high. The fountain springs into action after dark, shooting choreographed jets of water into the air which 'dance' in time to a range of Arabic, Hindi and classical music, while multicoloured lights play across the watery plumes. The magnificent shows are staged every 20 minutes between 6pm and 10pm in the evening (until 11pm Thur–Sat) and can be watched for free from anywhere around the lake and from some outlets in nearby Souk Al Bahar.

## Old Town and Souk Al Bahar

Return to the rear exit of The Dubai Mall, where you exited the mall, then turn right across the small footbridge to reach 'Old Town Island'. This is part of the extensive **Old Town** development: a swathe of low-rise, sand-coloured buildings with traditional Moorish styling. This area is atmospheric, particular-ly when lit up at night, with paved areas for pedestrians to walk along, making it one of the easier places to explore on foot.

On the far side of the footbridge lies **Souk Al Bahar ⑭** ('Souk of the Sailor'; Sat–Thur 10am–10pm, Fri 2–10pm), a small, Arabian-themed mall with a small selection of stores selling traditional handicrafts, and a few independent fashion outlets. Restaurants line the waterfront terrace outside, offering views of the Burj Khalifa and Dubai Fountain after dark.

On the far side of the Souk Al Bahar stands the opulent **The Palace – The Old Town ⑮** *(see p.110)*, its sumptuous Moorish-style façade and richly decorated interior offering a surreal contrast to the futuristic needle of the Burj Khalifa rising directly behind it. For food, the hotel's stylish **Thiptara** restaurant (see ⑪④), *p.52)* offers a memorable venue for an upmarket evening meal.

**Above from far left:** the Bastakiya area is known for its traditional architecture.

---

## Business Bay

Stretching south of Downtown Dubai, you can't fail to notice the burgeoning high-rises of Business Bay, the latest in Dubai's ongoing series of mega-developments which is steadily transforming yet another slice of quiet desert into a new, high-rise city-within-the-city.

Designed around an extension of the Dubai Creek, this vast new project is expected to come into service from 2012 onwards, with a huge mass of skyscrapers including the landmark Emirates Park Towers 1 and 2, the second-tallest buildings in Dubai at 376m (1,233ft). For the time being, the best way of seeing the development is from the Dubai Metro, as the elevated track offers marvellous views of the sometimes surreal new structures mushrooming up on every side.

**Tall Claims**
Dubai is purported to have the world's four tallest hotels: in order, the Rose Rayhaan (333m), Burj Al Arab (321m), Jumeirah Emirates Tower (309m) and The Address Downtown Dubai (306m), although all these will be overtaken by the two new Emirates Park Towers (376m) in Business Bay, due to open sometime in 2011–12.

# 5

# JUMEIRA

*This day-long tour starts with a visit to the Jumeira Mosque and a walk through the affluent expat suburbs before heading south to the spectacular Burj Al Arab and Madinat Jumeirah – two of modern Dubai's most memorable attractions.*

**Dress Appropriately**
In addition to dressing appropriately, before entering the mosque, you will be required to remove your shoes and enter in your bare feet, as is the custom. You should also remove your shoes at the Cultural Centre.

---

**DISTANCE** 14km (8.7 miles)
**TIME** A full day
**START** Jumeira Mosque
**END** Madinat Jumeirah
**POINTS TO NOTE**
Take a taxi to reach the starting point of the tour at Jumeira Mosque; you'll also need to catch cabs for short hops down the coastal road at various points; none should cost more than around Dhs10–15.

---

One of Dubai's wealthiest residential areas, **Jumeira** is home to many of the city's rich expat executives and their tanned and manicured wives (popularly, if rather disparagingly, known as 'Jumeira Janes'). Most of the area is decidedly suburban, although there are a number of attractions, including assorted beaches, malls, restaurants and cafés, while the neighbouring district of Umm Suqeim is home to a cluster of landmark attractions, including the iconic Burj Al Arab hotel.

## Jumeira Mosque

The tour begins at the striking **Jumeira Mosque ❶**. This is also the only mosque in Dubai that non-Muslims can visit via tours run by the **Sheikh Mohammed Centre for Cultural Understanding** (tel: 04 353 6666; www.cultures.ae; tours Sat, Sun, Tue and Thur 10am). Tours begin with entertaining and informative talks by a local Emirati guide after which the floor is thrown open to questions. There's no need to book, but you should be at the mosque 15 minutes before the tour starts. For a drink or early lunch after your tour, head for either **Japengo Café** (see ⑪①) or **Lime Tree Café** (see ⑪②), both within a stone's throw of the mosque.

## Jumeira Road

From the mosque, the seafront Jumeira Road arrows straight down the coast all the way to the end of the tour at the Madinat Jumeirah. The section of road immediately south of the mosque is lined with a series of small and rather old-fashioned malls – the best is the **Village Mall ❷** (www.thevillagedubai.com; Sat–Thur 10am–10pm, Fri 4pm–10pm), home to a few interesting fashion boutiques.

Heading down any of the side roads on the west side of Jumeira Road

brings you to **Jumeira Public Beach ❸** – a spacious expanse of free sand, although much less attractive than Jumeira Beach Park *(see below)* further down the road. It's about 1km down the road from the mosque to the Dubai Zoo; a rather boring walk, and worth avoiding by catching a cab (Dhs10). Alternatively, you may decide to skip the zoo altogether and head straight for the Mercato mall.

*Dubai Zoo*

Founded in 1967, the **Dubai Zoo ❹** (daily except Tue, 10am–6pm; Dhs2) is the oldest zoo on the Arabian peninsula, although it's very much looking its age, with overcrowded pens housing a motley assortment of random animals including giraffes, tigers, lions, chimps and brown bears, as well as local species including Arabian wolves and oryx.

*Mercato*

The largest of the various malls lining this part of Jumeira Road, the quirky **Mercato ❺** (daily 10am–10pm, Thur–Sat until midnight; www.mercatoshoppingmall.com) is well worth a look for its kitsch but entertaining décor. The whole place is designed to resemble a miniature Italian city, with a long central atrium lined by a balconied palazzi and side-alleys heading off to a pair of intimate plazas on either side – a nice spot for a quiet coffee. There's a good selection of upmarket boutiques too, aimed squarely at the wealthy local expat set.

*Jumeira Beach Park and Shoreside*

Around 2km south of Mercato, **Shoreside Complex ❻** *(see p.21)*, offers a stretch of rather expensive beach, while adjacent **Jumeira Beach Park ❼** *(see p.21)* is the most attractive public beach in the city, and well worth the modest admission fee. **Shu** (see 🍴③), opposite the entrance to the park, is a good spot for lunch.

Above from far left: the ornate domes of the Jumeira Mosque; alfresco dining at the Limetree Cafe.

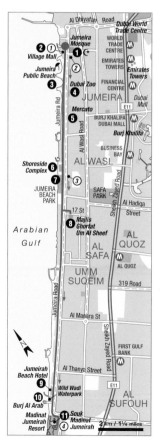

Above: gold horses, Mercato mall and a popular supermarket.

*Majlis Ghorfat Um Al Sheef*

Hop in a cab and continue south along the coastal Jumeira Road for another 2km until you reach 17 Street on your left where a large brown sign points to the venerable old **Majlis Ghorfat Um Al Sheef** ❽ (tel: 04 394 6343; Sat–Thur 8.30am–8.30pm, Fri 2.30–8.30pm; charge), 100m down the road on your left. Originally constructed in 1955, the two-storey majlis (meeting room) offers a touching throwback to earlier and simpler times, with its traditional coral stone walls, shady verandahs and teak doors. The majlis was originally the summer resort for Dubai's former ruler Sheikh Rashid,

serving as the venue for many meetings where the sheikh plotted Dubai's transformation from Arabian backwater to international super-city.

## UMM SUQEIM

South of the Majlis Ghorfat Um Al Sheef you enter the suburb of **Umm Suqeim** (although the entire area is usually, if inaccurately, referred to as Jumeira), home to three of Dubai's most famous modern landmarks.

*Jumeirah Beach Hotel*

Opened in 1997, the vast **Jumeirah Beach Hotel** ❾ (or 'JBH' as it's often

**Madinat Jumeirah**
Thai architect Thanu Boonyawatana likened his approach to that of a movie special effects wizard, who, with the aid of computer-generated imagery, recreates ancient Greece or Rome for cinema audiences. 'We thought, 'What if in ancient UAE or ancient Oman they had the money we have now and the technology we have now? We built what they might have built…'

---

## Food and Drink

### ① JAPENGO CAFÉ
Palm Strip Shopping Mall, Jumeira Road; tel: 04 343 5028; Fri–Wed 10am–1am, Thur 10am–2am; $$
Chic modern café-restaurant, with a shamelessly eclectic menu featuring everything from sushi and sashimi, through to stir fries, pizzas and lamb chops. You'll also find a good selection of sandwiches and salads. There's another branch overlooking the canal in the Souk Madinat Jumeirah.

### ② LIME TREE CAFÉ
Near Spinneys, Jumeira Road; tel: 04 349 8498; daily 7.30am–6pm; $–$$
Set in an attractive modern villa, this neat little café offers a classic slice of expat Jumeira life. Healthy specialities include outstanding carrot cake, tasty wraps and delicious smoothies.

### ③ SHU
Jumeira Road, opposite Jumeirah Beach Park; tel: 04 349 1303; Sun–Thur 10am–2am; $$
Chic Lebanese café with seating either in the cool interior or the relaxed outside terrace. If you're feeling adventurous, try the house speciality: fried sparrow with pomegranate syrup.

### ④ AL MAKAN
Souk Madinat Jumeirah; tel: 04 368 6593; www.alkoufa.com; daily noon–1am; $$
Al Makan offers a rare chance to sample authentic Emirati cuisine in a restaurant setting, along with a good selection of Lebanese mezze and grills. Outdoor terrace seating overlooks Burj Al Arab hotel.

known) was the first of the city's mega-hotels, a 100m (328ft-) high colossus built in the form of a gigantic breaking wave (although from some angles it looks more like a kind of rollercoaster). The hotel was considered the last word in luxury when it was opened, and although it has since been overtaken by even more exclusive and upmarket hotels elsewhere in the city, it remains one of southern Dubai's most distinctive and engaging landmarks. Immediately behind the hotel lies the perennially popular **Wild Wadi waterpark** *(see p.21)*.

## BURJ AL ARAB

Towering over the coastline just beyond the JBH is the stupendous **Burj Al Arab**, opened in 1999. Inspired by the shape of a huge, billowing sail, this marvellous high-rise hotel is far and away Dubai's most memorable modern landmark, its hugely distinctive, instantly recognisable outline providing the city with a defining landmark to rival the Eiffel Tower, Sydney Opera House or Big Ben.

The building is now home to the city's most exclusive hotel, popularly dubbed the world's first 'seven-star' hotel on account of the super-fuelled levels of luxury provided to guests in the hotels 200-odd suites. Access to the interior is limited to hotel guests or those with a confirmed reservation at one of the hotel's alluring but expensive bars and restaurants, although it's worth the cash to have a look at the remarkable interior with its cavernous,

multicoloured atrium, decorated in huge swathes of gold, red and blue.

## MADINAT JUMEIRAH

Immediately south of the Burj Al Arab rises the mighty **Madinat Jumeirah** complex, opened in 2004. The resort is a sight to behold; built in a form of a self-contained faux-Arabian city, its huge sand-coloured buildings topped with innumerable wind towers and criss-crossed with miniature canals.

Centrepiece of the complex is the lovely **Souk Madinat Jumeirah**, a superb mock-Arabian bazaar with winding alleyways lined with upmarket handicraft shops under elaborate wooden roofs and hanging lanterns. At the far end of the souk, a series of terraces tumble down to the canal below, lined with restaurants and bars, including the excellent **Al Makan** restaurant (see ⑪④).

Either side of the souk are the opulent buildings of the complex's two main hotels. To the north, the stunning **Mina A'Salam**, and to the south the even more opulent **Al Qasr**, well worth a visit for its spectacular foyer, with vast chandeliers, burbling fountains and vast quantities of marble.

**Above from far left**
Jumeirah Beach Hotel; the interior of the Burj Al Arab; traditional architecture.

# DUBAI MARINA AND PALM JUMEIRAH

*The southern end of the city is characterised by its modern developments: high-rise Dubai Marina and Palm Jumeirah, the world's largest man-made island.*

**DISTANCE** 25km (15.5 miles)
**TIME** Half-day/full day
**START** The Walk, JBR
**END** One&Only Mirage, Dubai Marina
**POINTS TO NOTE**
You could easily spend a full day exploring the places described here if you decide to devote some time to the various in-house attractions at the Atlantis resort, including a visit to the Aquaventure waterpark and Dolphin Bay. If not, you could get around everywhere in about half a day, at a push. In terms of transport, you'll need to catch several cabs to get between the places described below, although depending on where you're staying you can possibly save money by catching the metro down to Dubai Marina station at the beginning of the tour and catching a cab from there to the starting point, and then taking the metro back from the same station at the end of the day.

Bounding the southern end of the city is the vast new **Dubai Marina** development (or 'New Dubai', as it's sometimes called). This entire dis-trict is effectively a brand new city-within-the-city: a swathe of densely packed skyscrapers which have mushroomed out of the desert with magical rapidity over the past five or so years. Even by Dubai standards, the speed and scale of the develop-ment here is astonishing, especially for those who remember this part of Dubai in its earlier days, when the entire area was little more than desert, bar a modest line of hotels fringing the coast.

### The Walk, Jumeirah Beach Residence

For tourists, the heart of the Marina remains the string of upmarket beach-side hotels which line the coast on the western side of the area, fronting onto a long expanse of fine white-sand beach. The entire area along the beachfront between the Sheraton and Le Royal Meridien hotels has now been developed as **The Walk, Jumeirah Beach Residence ❶**, JBR (as it is often called). A residential area with an attractive pedestrianised promenade, The Walk runs along the back of the beach and is dotted with dozens of cafés, restaurants and a few shops including the popular high-end

department store, Boutique 1. It's also home to the lively Covent Garden Market (www.coventgardenmarket.ae; Oct–April Wed & Thur 5pm–midnight, Fri & Sat 10am–9pm), during which dozens of stalls selling clothes, jewellery and other collectables by local and expat craftsmen, designers and artists are set up along the promenade.

## Dubai Marina Beach

Right next to The Walk, the extensive **Dubai Marina Beach ❷** is one of the finest in the city, with a good swathe of broad white sand. Most of the beach has now been colonized by the various hotels, although a section of free public beach survives between the Sheraton and Hilton hotels. It's also possible to use the beaches, pools and other facilities at many of the hotels for a (usually rather steep) fee *(see p.20)*. Watersports centres can also be found at nearly all the Marina beach hotels (apart from the Ritz-Carlton), offering various activities including sailing, windsurfing, kayaking, wakeboarding, water-skiing and parasailing.

## Marina Walk

Stroll to the north end of The Walk, turning up past Le Royal Meridien and Habtoor Grand hotels, then (carefully) cross the main road and go down the side of the Marriott hotel. This brings you onto the far end of the impressive **Marina Walk ❸**, an expansive pedestrian promenade which runs around the edge of the

Dubai Marina, lined with a long string of further cafés and restaurants. **Zaatar W Zeit** café (see ⑪①), serves up fast food with a Lebanese twist, and is a good lunch option. The Marina itself is a man-made sea inlet, around 1.5km long, dotted with luxury yachts and hemmed in by a positive forest of skyscrapers. It's an impressive sight, although the haphazard layout of the entire area, with random

Above:
A glamorous selection of yachts in the Marina.

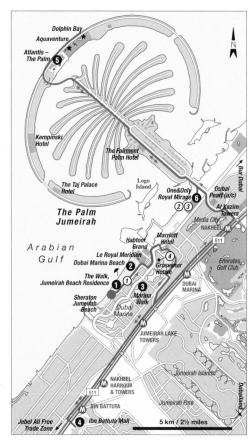

**Above from left:**
The elaborate ceiling inside Ibn Battuta Mall; the trunk of the Palm Jumeirah, the main route through the development and to Atlantis The Palm; shoppers at Ibn Battuta Mall.

high-rises crammed pell-mell into every available space, serves as a chastening memorial to the super-fuelled property boom of the mid-noughties – and from whose after-effects the city is still recovering.

### Ibn Battuta Mall

Continue around the Marina Walk, then, when you've seen enough, take any of the side roads exiting the marina to your left and catch a cab for the 4km ride (around Dhs15) down to the **Ibn Battuta Mall** ❹ (www.ibn battutamall.com; daily 10am–10pm,

Wed–Fri until midnight), situated in something of a no-man's land at the far southern end of the city, close to the sprawling industrial works and container docks of the Jebel Ali Free Trade Zone.

The mall is one of the city's most outlandish but engaging attractions, inspired by the travels of the famous Moroccan wanderer Ibn Battuta, with different sections themed after six of the many countries and regions he visited – Morocco, Andalucia, Tunisia, Persia, India and China – all designed with Dubai's characteristic

**The Big City**
Dubai is now far and away the tallest city on the planet, home to no less than 18 of the world's 100 tallest buildings, outstripping traditional skyscraper cities like New York (with eight buildings in the top hundred) and Hong Kong (with six). Pride of place goes to the cloud-capped Burj Khalifa *(see p.53)*, the world's tallest building, while other high-rise landmarks include the Burj Al Arab *(see p.59)*, the glittering Emirates Towers (see p.49), and the Rose Reyhaan *(see p.51)*, the world's tallest hotel.

## Food and Drink 🍽

**① ZAATAR W ZEIT**
The Walk, JBR; daily 10am–midnight; $
Cheery Lebanese-style fast food, with salads, wraps and pizzas alongside various kinds of manakish (a kind of Middle Eastern-style pizza) and other Lebanese-style snacks.

**② NINA'S**
Arabian Courtyard, One&Only Royal Mirage; tel: 04 399 9999;
Mon–Sat 7–11.30pm $$$$
Innovative modern Indian restaurant, combining subcontinental flavours with International ingredients and cooking techniques – anything from traditional butter chicken through to frogs' legs and rambutan.

**③ TAGINE**
The Palace, One&Only Royal Mirage tel: 04 399 9999;
Tue–Sun 7–11.30pm; $$$$
This exquisitely decorated little Moroccan restaurant is one of the most appealing in the city, with Arabian Nights décor and a fine range of traditional Moroccan cuisine, including a delicious selection of tagines, spicy *harira* (soup), lamb's brain and pigeon pie.

**④ BUDDHA BAR**
Grosvenor House, Dubai Marina; tel: 04 317 6000;
daily 7.30pm–midnight; $$$$
One of the Dubai's most impressive restaurants. The swanky eatery is modelled after its famous Parisian namesake, and it offers a fine selection of Japanese, Thai and Chinese dishes.

mix of whimsy, extravagance and high-end kitsch. Highlights include the bright red Chinese court, with a life-size junk, the elaborate Indian section complete with a large plaster elephant and mechanical mahout, a Tunisian village at twilight, and the marvellously decorated Persian section, centred on a huge domed courtyard reminiscent more of a grand mosque than the atrium of a local shopping centre.

## PALM JUMEIRAH

From the Ibn Battuta Mall, hop in a cab for the 16km ride (around Dhs25) back across the Marina to Atlantis, at the far end of **Palm Jumeirah.** The ride back north through the tangled skyscrapers of the Dubai Marina is worth the price alone.

Past the Al Kazim Towers, you'll turn left onto the approach road to the vast Palm Jumeirah artificial island, first opened in 2006, although work is still progressing on the string of five-star hotels (including new Taj, Kempinski and Fairmont resorts) which will eventually line the outermost stretch of the island. Billed as the 'Eighth Wonder of the World', the Palm is currently the world's largest man-made island, and has doubled the length of the Dubai coastline at a cost of around $12 billion.

Designed in the form of a palm tree, the drive onto the island, along the main road, runs down the central 'trunk' of the tree (adding a whole new dimension to the expression 'trunk road'), 16 fronds (each guarded by a security checkpoint) fan out either side, lined with luxury villas, each with their own little slice of private beach at the end of their gardens.

Unfortunately, you can only really appreciate the unique layout of the island from the air; from the ground, the whole thing looks like suburban clutter, while the architecture along the main trunk road is decidedly humdrum, at least until you approach the far end of the island, when the grandiose Atlantis The Palm resort looms ahead.

*Atlantis The Palm*

At the far end of the Palm, the large façade of **Atlantis The Palm** ❺ (www.atlantisthepalm.com) rears into view above the seafront. The resort is

## Dubai's Artificial Islands

Palm Jumeirah has already added 68km to the emirate's coastline, although this is just the first of four proposed offshore developments, intended to create up to 500km of new waterfront. Two further palm-shaped islands are already in the pipeline: the Palm Jebel Ali, 20km further down the coast, and the gargantuan Palm Deira, right next to the city centre. Both are currently stalled due to financial difficulties, although large-scale reclamation works have already been finished.

Even more fanciful is the extravagant The World development, a vast complex of artificial islands constructed in the approximate shape of a map of the world, with many of the world's countries represented by their own islands (larger countries have been subdivided into several islands), but as with many mega projects in Dubai, development of the islands has halted in the wake of the global financial crisis

an almost identikit copy of its sister establishment, the Atlantis Paradise Island resort in the Bahamas, with the addition of the few discrete Islamic touches, looking like some enormous Disney palace, although despite the sheer size of the place, it lacks the quirky charm and opulent detailing of other modern developments in the city.

Inside, the hotel is as unabashedly over-the-top, as one would probably expect. Entering the main foyer, you're confronted by Dale Chihuly's extraordinary installation in the lobby – a towering glass sculpture looking like a huge waterfall of blue, green, pink and orange noodles. From here, corridors stretch away in either direction, lined with fat gold columns and vast chandeliers, while a floor-to-ceiling viewing panel offers spectacular glimpses into the vast aquarium of the hotel's Lost Chambers (see below).

### The Lost Chambers

Atlantis boasts a host of (expensive) in-house attractions. Inside the hotel itself, the kooky **Lost Chambers** (daily 10am–11pm; Dhs100; children under 12, Dhs70) seems to consist of the remains of the legendary city of Atlantis itself, featuring a sequence of underwater halls and tunnels, dotted with specially constructed 'ruins'. This is Dubai at its most shamelessly cheesy, although you may enjoy the sheer absurdity of the idea, and the view of approximately 65,000 resident fish, large and small, swimming around the submerged faux-classical remains.

### Aquaventure and Dolphin Bay

In the grounds outside you'll find the resort's spectacular **Aquaventure** waterpark, home to a pulse-quickening selection of water coasters, slides and power jets, plus the massive Ziggurat which holds the nail-biting Leap of Faith waterslide, which drops those brave enough to tackle it at stomach-churning speeds down into a plastic tunnel in the middle of a lagoon full of sharks. There are also various gentler activities for kids, while visitors can also use the fine stretch of private beach next door. Admission costs Dhs200 (Dhs165 for children under 1.2m; or Dhs250/200 adults/children including The Lost Chambers; free to in-house guests).

Next door, **Dolphin Bay** offers the chance to swim with the hotel's troupe of resident bottlenose dolphins. Shallow-water interactions cost Dhs790, deep-water interactions (over 12s only) Dhs975, plus observer passes (Dhs300; only available to visitors accompanying those taking part in full interactions). The hefty price tag also includes same-day admission to Aquaventure and the private beach.

### Back to the Marina

There are a number of upmarket restaurants within Atlantis The Palm, though it's worth returning to the mainland after dark and sampling some of the Marina nightlife, which boasts a slew of excellent, and generally much more affordable (though still not exactly cheap), places to eat and

drink. The best place to head for is the magestic **One&Only Royal Mirage** ❻, a captivating, Moorish-style resort which sprawls down the coast for the best part of a kilometre, wrapped in thousands of palm-trees and particularly impressive after dark. Restaurants here include the innovative **Nina's** (see ⑪②) and the opulent **Tagine** (see ⑪③). Alternatively, head for the chic **Grosvenor House Hotel**, home to a further collection of alluring places to eat and drink, including the memorable **Buddha Bar** (see ⑪④).

## DUBAILAND

Some 10km inland from the Marina lies the vast new **Dubailand** development (www.dubailand.ae). Launched in 2003, Dubailand was originally planned to be nothing less than the world's largest and most spectacular tourist development, with an mind-boggling mix of theme parks and sporting and leisure facilities – twice the size of the Walt Disney World Resort in Florida. Major attractions were to have included a massive waterpark and snowdome; the Great Dubai Wheel; the Restless Planet dinosaur theme park (with animatronic dinosaurs); the Falcon City of Wonders, with full-scale replicas of the seven wonders of the world; plus the world's largest mall (the Mall of Arabia) and biggest hotel (Asia-Asia, with a cool 6,500 rooms).

Parts of complex are already open, including the Dubai Autodrome and Dubai Sports City, complete with international cricket stadium and Ernie Els golf course. Work on other projects, however, has come to an end indefinitely, and whether any of Dubailand's more ambitious projects will now ever see the light of day is anyone's guess.

**Below:**
A 3D display revving up interest in Dubailand.

# CREEK CRUISES

*For a magical way to view the emirate, step on board a traditional dhow or abra and enjoy a breezy ride on the waters of the Creek and optimum views of the old city centre.*

**TIME** 1–2 hours
**START/END** Dubai Creek
**POINTS TO NOTE**

Take a taxi from your hotel to the starting point for your *dhow* cruise on Dubai Creek (operators are based in various locations). Companies such as Net Tours (tel: 04 266 6655) and Tour Dubai (tel: 04 336 8407) can pick you up from your hotel. It is best to book your *dhow* cruise at least one day in advance to avoid disappointment.

One of the best ways of exploring the Creek is either by chartering your own *abra* or by going on a dinner cruise aboard one of the dozens of traditional wooden *dhows* which ply the waters after dark. This is one of the best ways to enjoy the old city, with marvellous views of the surrounding Creekside buildings, with their eclectic tangle of traditional wind-towered buildings, soaring minarets and futuristic high-rises, as well as offering a closer look at the dozens of venerable old wooden *dhows* which still motor sedately up and down the Creek.

**What's In A Name?**
The name '*dhow*' comes from the Swahili word for boat, *dau*.

**Cruising The Creek**
Notable landmarks on a cruise along the Creek include the National Bank of Dubai *(see p.33)* and the clubhouse of the Dubai Creek Golf Club *(see p.42)*, as well as the water-facing side of Bur Dubai Old Souk *(see p.28)*, with its marvellous old coral stone buildings.

### Abra tours

As well as the short five-minute hop across the Creek by traditional *abra (see p.28)*, it's also possible to charter one of these old-fashioned boats for longer tours up and down the Creek. Chartering an *abra* costs Dhs100 per hour, and the drivers will take you wherever you fancy. An hour's cruise will allow you to ride from the city centre down to the Dubai Creek Golf Club and back again. To find an *abra* for hire, head to the nearest *abra* station and ask around. Note that the rate of Dhs100 per hour is officially fixed (and posted in writing at all *abra* stations) and the same regardless of how many people use the boat, so don't be hassled into paying more. Take whatever food and drink you might need with you.

### Dhow cruises

A more comfortable alternative to chartering an *abra* is to go on one of the ever-popular evening **dinner cruises** – these can be booked through any of the city's tour operators, while many hotels can also arrange trips. Most cruises are aboard traditional old wooden *dhows*, offering a leisurely overview of the city. Cruises generally last two hours, departing at around 8–8.30pm and cost anything from Dhs120 to Dhs350 depending on who you go with, inclusive of a buffet dinner.

Independent cruise operators include Rikks Cruises (tel: 04 357 2200, www.rikks.net), which offers some of the cheapest cruises in town, and the more upmarket Al Mansour Dhow, operated by the Radisson Blu hotel (tel: 04 205 7333).

For a more modern alternative Bateaux Dubai (tel: 04 399 4994) runs cruises in its state-of-the-art glass-sided modern boat, offering a touch more luxury than other operators, plus better-than-average food. Alternatively, Danat Dubai Cruises (tel: 04 351 1117) run upmarket cruises along the Creek and also out along the coast aboard their state-of-the-art catamaran.

**Above from far left:** all set for diners, on board a *dhow*; workman repairing a *dhow*.

**The Arabian *Dhow***
The design of the traditional dhows you see plying the waters of the Creek today are little changed from a hundred years past, although today's boats now rely on modern engine-power rather than the oars and distinctive triangular 'lateen' sails of yesteryear.

## Medieval Ships

The daring and prowess of medieval Arab sailors has become the stuff of legend, inspiring the legendary tales of Sinbad the Sailor and many other mariners' yarns. At the height of Gulf trade, in the 9th century, Gulf seamen were sailing all the way to China, sometimes making massive profits en route, although often experiencing hair-raising shipwrecks and other maritime misadventures and mishaps en route. Despite the romantic legends, the life of the medieval Arab seaman was a hard one, spending days and nights exposed to the elements, often in conditions of extreme hardship. Crew were expected to accommodate themselves as best they could on top of the cargo, while ablutions were carried out in a precarious box slung out over the side of the boat. Most seafaring boats were surprisingly small, built using the traditional 'sewn' construction, with the planks of boats not nailed but literally stitched together using coconut twine, caulked with a mixture of coir and fish oil, a mode of ship building that came as a constant surprise to Europeans and Arabs from the Mediterranean, such as Marco Polo and Ibn Battuta.

# DESERT ADVENTURE

*No visit to Dubai is complete without a foray into the desert, which stretches inland to the south of the city, offering a brief taste of the mighty sands which cover most of the Arabian Peninsula.*

**Above:** desert blooms; local hazard.

**Below:** spectacular sand dunes.

---

**DISTANCE** 150km (93 miles) round trip
**TIME** A half or full day
**START/END** Central Dubai
**POINTS TO NOTE**

Unless you have lots of experience off-road driving in desert conditions, the best way to see the desert properly is to book a safari with a licensed tour operator. For obvious reasons (there aren't any) restaurants aren't mentioned on the route. If you're part of an organised tour, all food and drinks will be provided en route (and afternoon safaris typically culminate in a lavish buffet dinner at a desert camp). If you're travelling independently, take whatever food you're likely to need, plus large amounts of water – it's easy to get seriously dehydrated in the desert heat.

---

Trips into the desert are most conveniently arranged by signing up for a trip with one of Dubai's tour operators – most tours put the emphasis firmly on a stereotypical mish-mash of dune-bashing, belly-dancing and other touristy crowd-pleasers, although there are some more rewarding (and peaceful) alternatives available if you shop around. The best time to experience the desert is late in the afternoon, when the light is as soft and warm as the sand underfoot, while after dark the night sky, away from any ambient light, is remarkably clear.

Around 65 per cent of the 85,000 sq km (33,000 sq miles) of the UAE is desert. The term encompasses a variety of landscapes and conditions: as well as rolling dunes, it includes salt flats *(sabkha)*, flood plains, mountains and river valleys. The

desert that begins on the outskirts of Dubai (or more accurately within the city limits, where every vacant lot is sandy) forms part of the Saharo-Arabian Desert, the most extensive dry zone in the world, which stretches away into Oman and Saudi Arabia, covering most of the Arabian peninsula. Not surprisingly, the further you get from Dubai, the more unspoilt the scenery becomes – sadly, much of the desert in the immediate vicinity of the city has been more or less ruined by huge highways, petrol stations, looming pylons and swathes of random development.

## Big Red

The most popular desert destination close to Dubai is the complex by a large dune, next to the main highway 44, about halfway between Dubai and the Hatta road. It is popularly known as '**Big Red' ❶**, this huge mountain of sand is impressive at any time of day, but particularly magical towards dusk, when the low light turns it to a rich, russet red. Unfortunately, the dunes' natural majesty are somewhat compromised by the hoardes of four-wheel drives and quad bikes which can be seen at pretty much any time of day struggling up and down the dunes' steep sides, like hyperactive ants. The slightly smaller (but still mightily impressive) swathe of dunes on the opposite side of the highway is a popular dune-bashing destination for local tour companies.

## Dubai Desert Conservation Reserve

For a much more peaceful desert experience, the best place to head is the superb **Dubai Desert Conservation Reserve ❷** (www.ddcr.org), around 45km (28 miles) from Dubai next to the main E66 highway to Al Ain. The reserve encloses 250km of low, shifting dunes, dotted with

**Above from far left:**
4x4 on the road; watch out for sand dunes; vegetation for the dry climate; hot-air ballooning offers a spectacular way of viewing the desert.

**Be Prepared**
Although generally not as humid as the coast, the desert is, of course, extremely hot during the day. Make sure you pack plenty of liquid refreshments, sun cream and a hat, and if you are going to be out after sunset, pack a jumper – without cloud cover to trap the heat of the day, Arabian nights can be surprisingly chilly.

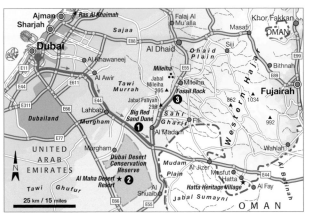

**Above:** local men enjoying a stroll through the desert.

hardy ghaf trees, and serves as a refuge for over thirty local species of mammal and reptile, including rare creatures such as the oryx, Arabian gazelle, sand gazelle, Arabian red fox and sand fox. Access to the reserve is carefully controlled. The cheapest option is to come on a visit with one of the select group of Dubai tour operators who are allowed to run tours here (including Arabian Adventures). Alternatively, you can stay in the reserve at the idyllic, but spectacularly expensive, **Al Maha** resort *(see p.113)*.

*Fossil Rock*

Another popular desert destination is **Fossil Rock** ❸, part of the craggy Jebel Mileiha – an impressive lump of rock standing in splendid isolation amidst the sands and looking a bit like an enormous decaying tooth. The rock is named after the marine-life fossils that can be found in it, proof that these rocks (like many in this part of the UAE and Oman) were formed underwater. The rock lies around 50km (31 miles) from Dubai, just south of the road to Khor Kalba and Fujairah.

## Desert Tours

By far the easiest way to explore the desert is with one of Dubai's numerous specialist tour companies, most of whom offer a range of half-day, full-day and overnight trips. These usually feature some dune-bashing (speeding over the dunes in a four-wheel-drive) and perhaps one or two other activities like sand-skiing or quad-biking, followed by an evening barbecue at a cheesy 'traditional' tented camp with belly-dancer, camel ride, henna-painting and so on. For a more peaceful view of the desert, it's worth spending a night under canvas. A few operators also offer less stereotypical desert trips, perhaps with visits to a local village, date plantation or camel farm.

Dubai's leading operator is Arabian Adventures (tel: 04 303 4888; www.arabian-adventures.com), a professional and well-run outfit offering a wide range of tours, although usually at slightly higher prices than other places. Other reliable operators include Alpha Tours (tel: 04 294 9888, www.alphatours dubai.com), Net Tours (tel: 04 602 8888, www.nettoursdubai.com) and Orient Tours (tel: 04 282 8238; www.orienttours.ae).

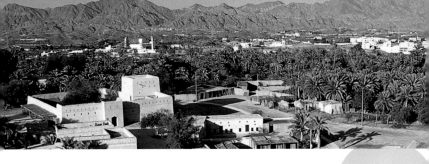

# HATTA

*This is a one- or two-day trip into the Hajar Mountains and Hatta, with its fort and springs. Avoid going on Fridays and public holidays, when the track to Hatta Pools is clogged with 4x4s. If you want to stay overnight, the Hatta Fort Hotel is recommended.*

Some 110km (68 miles) from Dubai (around an hour's drive along the modern Highway 44) lies rural **Hatta** ❶. Hatta is a small enclave of Dubai territory, surrounded by land belonging to Oman, Ras Al Khaimah and Ajman, but visitors do not need passports or visas to enter the area and there are no checkpoints to pass through. The border post for Oman is actually 10km (6 miles) further to the east of Hatta.

To reach Hatta from central Dubai, take route 44. The first sign that you are nearing Hatta is the sight of roadside carpet stalls, followed by the hilltop summer homes that belong to Dubai's sheikhs and wealthy businessmen. When you reach the roundabout with an open-sided fortress in the middle, either turn left for Hatta Fort Hotel, or right for Hatta Heritage Village and the road to Hatta Pools.

## HERITAGE VILLAGE

**Hatta Heritage Village** ❷ (tel: 04 851 1374; Sat–Thur 8.30am–8.30pm, Fri 2.30–8.30pm; free) brings the community's colourful history to life. Various styles of mountain dwellings have been rebuilt around carefully restored buildings, including the first

**DISTANCE** 250km (155 miles) round trip
**TIME** A full day or overnight
**START/END** Hatta
**POINTS TO NOTE**
Regular buses run between Dubai and Hatta (daily 6am–9pm; hourly from the Gold Souk Bus Station, Deira). To explore the surrounding area, however, you should rent a car (see p.106).

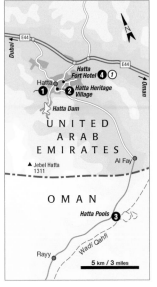

**Above:** Hatta Heritage Village viewed from its defensive watchtower.

**Prehistoric Hatta**
Archaeological finds have revealed that the fertile mountain valleys around Hatta were inhabited more than 4,000 years ago, during the Bronze Age. Excavations in the Juma valley have uncovered an ancient settlement and tombs similar to those found in Umm Al Nar, Abu Dhabi, dating from c.2,000–2,500BC. Finds from the site are displayed at Dubai Museum (see p.27).

fort in the emirate of Dubai, constructed in 1790, which now houses a weaponry museum. Check out the fascinating variety of mud and *barasti* (palm frond) houses and a restored *falaj* irrigation system that channels water through the village to the neighbourhood's date-palm gardens. On weekends and public holidays, local women in national dress and *burqa* face masks work away at traditional crafts (note that you should always ask their permission before snapping away). The watchtowers that loom high over the village date back to 1850.

## HATTA POOLS

The heritage village aside, Hatta's main attraction for many are the **Hatta Pools** ❸ and the off-road drive that continues beyond the pools through Wadi Qahfi to the Omani village of Rayy. The dirt track that leads to the pools begins several kilometres/miles from Hatta itself. The Hatta Fort Hotel *(see right)* can provide navigation sheets with directions and key landmarks to guests who have their own 4x4s. Alternatively, you might book a tour in a 4x4 through the hotel to share the expense of vehicle and driver with other guests.

### The Pools

Don't expect idyllic pools, cascading waterfalls and a brimming river at Hatta Pools and you won't be disappointed. The stunning but parched landscape around the pools bears

**Above:** watchtower near Hatta; beware of dry river beds; towards Hatta.

comparison with the surface of Mars. The access track is dusty, the river bed largely dry, while the spring pools are made up of low-level, slow-moving water. Throughout the year, there is enough water at crossing points to make a splash though.

## HATTA FORT HOTEL

The attractive **Hatta Fort Hotel** ❹ (PO Box 9277, Hatta; tel: 04 852 3211; www.hattaforthotel.com; is a venerable institution surrounded by dry, jagged, volcanic rock. The complex feels a bit like a safari lodge, with fine views over the surrounding mountains.

Even if you are not planning to stay the night, you can lunch at **Gazebo** (see ⑪①) or, for a nominal charge, relax by the pool.

## BACK TO DUBAI

To get back to Dubai, return to Hatta, then pick up route 44, which leads all the way back.

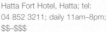

### Food and Drink
**① GAZEBO**
Hatta Fort Hotel, Hatta; tel: 04 852 3211; daily 11am–8pm; $$–$$$
Located on an air-conditioned balcony above the Hatta Fort Hotel's gorgeous swimming pool, Gazebo offers a marvellous view of the landscaped gardens and the rugged Hajar mountains beyond, backed up by a well-prepared selection of international dishes.

# SHARJAH

*Just 10km up the coast from Dubai, but light-years distant in terms of attitude and atmosphere, lies the conservative emirate of Sharjah, self-styled 'cultural capital' of the UAE, and home to an interesting range of museums devoted to the region's cultural and Islamic traditions.*

The UAE's third-largest emirate after Abu Dhabi and Dubai (population 750,000), Sharjah has a decidedly different flavour from neighbouring Dubai (even though, physically, the two cities have now more or less fused in a formless expanse of concrete). Compared to life in free-wheeling, liberal Dubai, Sharjah has clung much more firmly to its traditional cultural roots, exemplified by the fine string of museums which have been set up across the city, as well as by the total ban on alcohol and the more explicit adherence to Sharia-style law – conservative dress and behaviour are advised at all times.

## SHARJAH SOUK AND AROUND

At the western end of the city centre, close to the waterfront, stands the vast **Sharjah Souk** ❶ (also known as the Blue Souk, Central Souk and Souk Al Markasi). This is the largest souk in the UAE, housed in a striking pair of modern buildings topped with wind towers and embellished with blue tiles and traditional Islamic designs (although the rounded roof can be likened to a line of oil barrels lying side by side). Inside, the

**DISTANCE** 20km (12 miles)
**TIME** A full day
**START/END** Dubai
**POINTS TO NOTE**

The road between Dubai and Sharjah is perhaps the most notoriously congested in the UAE, usually descending into total gridlock during the morning and evening rush hours – it's best to travel to Sharjah after 10am (or perhaps slightly later) and return either before 5pm or after 8pm. Buses run 24hr (every 20–30min) from Al Ghubaiba Bus Station in Bur Dubai, dropping you at the bus station in Sharjah about 300m north of Central Souk, and about 750m from the Heritage Area. You might also be able to catch a cab, although many drivers are reluctant to take passengers to Sharjah due to the appalling traffic, and fares are subject to a Dhs20 surcharge. Expect the journey to take a minimum of 45min, potentially twice that during rush hours.

myriad of shops (Sat–Thur 10am–1pm and 4–10pm, closed Fri am) are spread over two levels, stuffed with a veritable treasure trove of carpets, antiques and

**Eastern Sharjah**
References to 'Sharjah', which means 'eastern' in Arabic, date to at least 1490, when the Arab navigator Ahmad Ibn Majid wrote that ships could find this area if they followed the stars from the island of Tunb.

Above from left:
Sharjah Heritage
Area; Sharjah
Cityscape; Heritage
area

assorted souvenirs. Those downstairs are devoted to every day items including perfumes, cheap shoes and electrical goods, while upstairs you'll find the souk's excellent spread of antique and carpet shops – if you're looking to buy a rug, this is the place to head, although bargaining is, of course, essential. The **Danial** restaurant (see ⑪①), just behind the souk in the Crystal Plaza, is a good place to or you to stop for food.

### Al Mahattah Museum

East of Sharjah Souk, King Abd Al Aziz Street was, until 1976, the main runway of the UAE's first airport, originally established in 1932 as a stopover for flights from London to Australia. The UAE's first hotel, the Fortress, just off King Abd Al Aziz Street, has been restored and, with an air-traffic control tower, forms the aviation-themed **Al**

**Mahattah Museum ❷** (tel: 06 573 3079, www.sharjahmuseums.ae; Sat–Thur 8am–8pm, Fri 4–8pm; charge), a 10-minute walk from Sharjah Souk. Among the aircraft on display are a World War II-era Avro Anson and a Douglas DC3, which belonged to the Gulf Aviation Co., the forerunner of Gulf Air.

## THE HERITAGE AREA

From Al Mahattah Museum, it's a 20-minute walk or short taxi ride (around Dhs10) to Sharjah's **Heritage Area**. This entire area of low-lying traditional houses has now been carefully restored and is home to a clutch of low-key museums and Souk Al Arsa.

### Souk Al Arsa

At the heart of the Heritage Area lies the **Souk Al Arsa ❸** (Sat–Thur 10am–1pm and 4.30–9pm, Fri 4.30–9pm), the UAE's oldest souk, and perhaps its prettiest, with dozens of traditional coral stone shops set around a miniature labyrinth of little alleyways beneath palm-frond roofs. Most of the shops here are devoted to antiques and handicrafts, with an interesting range of mainstream souvenirs and more unusual bric-a-bric for sale. The **Souk Al Arsah Coffee Shop** (see left, ⑪②) is a good place for lunch or a drink.

### Heritage Area Museums

Several museums stand close to Souk Al Arsa. Probably the most interesting is the **Bait Al Naboodah ❹** (tel: 06 568 1738, www.sharjahmuseums.ae;

**Sharjah Biennial**
Following the establishment of Sharjah Art Museum in 1995, the emirate has developed a reputation as a centre for the arts in the UAE. The city is also home to the celebrated Sharjah Biennial (www.sharjahbienniaI.org), held in odd-numbered years, it is a two-month show featuring work by international artists held at various venues around the city.

> ## Food and Drink 🍴
> ### ① DANIAL
> Crystal Plaza; daily 12.30pm–1.30am; $$
> Given the lack of places to eat in Sharjah Souk, this place (in the Crystal Plaza, immediately to the south) is a handy option, with reasonable buffet lunches and a selection of Middle Eastern and Iranian dishes.
>
> ### ② SOUK AL ARSAH COFFEE SHOP
> Souk Al Arsa, Heritage Area; daily 8am–10pm; $
> Cute little café on the pretty courtyard at the heart of the Souk Al Arsa – a good place to grab a drink or try one of the café's spicy chicken, mutton or fish birianis.

Sat–Thur 8am–8pm, Fri 4–8pm; charge), one of the finest traditional courtyard houses in the UAE, attractively restored with old wooden furniture and assorted artefacts.

Close by, the diminutive **Majlis of Ibrahim Mohammed Al Madfa ⑤** (tel: 06 568 1738, www.sharjah museums.ae; Sat–Thur 8am–8pm, Fri 4–8pm; free) is best known for its much-photographed round wind tower, the only one of its kind in the UAE. The house was formerly home of **Ibrahim Mohammed Al Madfa,** founder of the region's first newspaper in 1927 and one-time adviser to the ruling Al Qasimi family. The building, where Al Madfa once received business guests, now houses a tiny museum showcasing his personal effects.

## Ruler's Fort

Heading down any of the narrow streets which run east from the Heritage Area brings you to the wide Al Burj Avenue, running from Rolla Square down to the waterfront. Plum in the middle of the avenue sits **Al Hisn Fort ⑥** (tel: 06 568 5500, www.sharjahmuseums.ae; Tue–Thur, Sat–Sun 9am–1pm and 4–8pm, Fri 4–8pm; charge). The former city fort is an imposing old structure which formerly served as the residence of the ruling Al Qasimi family, although it now looks somewhat forlorn in the middle of a small canyon of banks and offices. The interior is home to an interesting museum focusing on the history of the city, although at the

**Sharjah Markets**

On the opposite side of the flyover from Sharjah's souk, there are markets specialising in fish, fruit and vegetables, and animals.

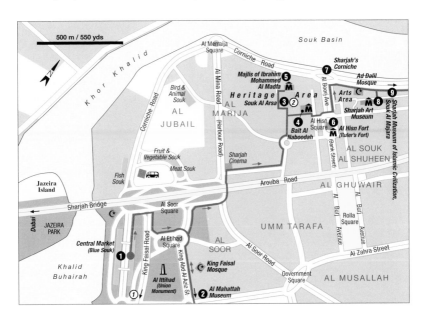

**Above:**
Sharjah Art Museum

time of writing it was closed for long-term renovations.

## ALONG THE CORNICHE

Continue along Al Burj Avenue to reach **Sharjah's Corniche ❼**. Like the waterfront in Deira, this is an impromptu harbour, usually with dozens of traditional wooden *dhow* moored up, and piles of merchandise cluttering the pavement – a fine sight.

### Sharjah Art Museum

Turn right along the Corniche and walk for five minutes, past the modern Iranian Souk, then turn right, away from the water, following the signs to the imposing **Sharjah Art Museum ❽** (tel: 06 568 8222, www.sharjah museums.ae; Sat–Thur 8am–8pm, Fri 4–8pm; charge). The main attraction here is the Orientalist section upstairs, devoted to a fine collection of paintings by 19th-European artists' depicting life in Islamic lands, including some memorable lithographs by Scottish artist David Roberts (1796–1864). The ground floor of the museum is devoted to temporary exhibitions, usually featuring local and/or Arab artists.

### Sharjah Museum of Islamic Civilization

Perhaps the highlight of the city is the world-class new **Sharjah Museum of Islamic Civilization ❾** (Sat–Thur 8am–8pm, Fri 4–8pm), a further five minutes' walk along the Corniche in the beautifully restored **Souk Al Majara**, topped with its distinctive golden dome. The ground floor of the museum offers a wide-ranging and excellently presented overview of the contributions made by Muslim scientists, artists and architects to world knowledge over the past 500 years, including absorbing displays on medieval Islamic chemistry, medicine, astronomy and navigation, backed up with quaint gadgets like armillary spheres, wall quadrants, astrolabes, equatoriums and waterclocks. Upstairs, four galleries showcase a wide range of superb Islamic arts and crafts, including beautiful historic manuscripts, ceramics, glass, armour, woodwork, textiles and jewellery.

## Religious Tolerance

According to the Sheikh Mohammed Centre for Cultural Understanding, 'Cultural and religious diversity has made the Emirates probably the most open and tolerant country within the region. Dubai and the UAE in general are liberal in allowing foreigners to maintain their own religious practices and lifestyles'. Although Emiratis are Muslims, and the legal system that applies to locals and foreigners alike is based on Islamic Sharia law, the Dubai Government allows people of other faiths to gather for worship, as long as they do not proselytise Muslims. A number of Christian churches have been established on land provided by the rulers on the Bur Dubai side of the Creek. As Friday is the local weekend, most churches have main services then – Sunday is a normal working day.

# THE NORTHERN EMIRATES

*The drive from Dubai through the northern emirates of Ajman, Umm Al Quwain and Ras Al Khaimah is like a journey back in time: the further you travel, the more you can envisage how Dubai looked before the oil boom – and how undeveloped other parts of the UAE remain even to this day.*

The northern emirates extend to Ras Al Khaimah, some 140km (87 miles) from Dubai. As you head north-east, away from Dubai, you pass through notably less-wealthy, less-populous and less-developed parts of the UAE.

## To Ajman

From Dubai, drive to Sharjah, aiming for Rolla Square and then turning left down Al Burj Avenue to reach the seafront corniche. From here, follow the corniche, passing the large Radisson SAS Hotel on your left, along a regal avenue of palm trees, wrought-iron railings and a showcase fountain signalling the presence of the Ruler's Palace, also on your left.

Continue along the coast road into the emirate of Ajman. This is a particularly attractive drive, with a long white-sand beach flanking the road on your left – a bit like a less developed version of Dubai's Jumeira coastline.

## AJMAN

Some 10km (6 miles) beyond Sharjah, a modest cluster of high-

> **DISTANCE** 162km (100 miles) round trip
> **TIME** A full day
> **START/END** Dubai
> **POINTS TO NOTE**
>
> A rental car (see p.106) is required for this itinerary. A good plan is to drive north following the coastal road through Sharjah, Ajman and Umm Al Quwain, and then return along the faster but much less scenic inland Emirates Road (E311). Whichever way you drive it's a long day-trip if you want to get all the way to Ras Al Khaimah – an early start is recommended. If you don't want to drive, some tour operators in Dubai run tours of Ajman and Ras Al Khaimah, covering most of the sights described below.

**Above:** a man with a camel on the beach in Ajman.

rises announces the arrival of Ajman itself. In terms of ambience, **Ajman** ❶ is much like the Dubai of the 1980s. The smallest of the UAE's seven emirates (250 sq km, 97 sq miles; population 275,000), Ajman has no oil wealth and continues to

rely on traditional industries such as boat-building and fishing.

### Ajman Museum

The main attraction here is the excellent **Ajman Museum** (tel: 06 742 3824; Sat–Thur 9am–1pm and 4–7pm, closed Fri; charge) in the town's old fort. To reach the museum, take a right turn at the Ajman Beach Hotel and follow the road alongside the edge of the pretty marina to Leewara Street. Turn right and, at the first roundabout, bear left towards Clocktower roundabout and Central Square. The fort will be to your left.

Built *c.*1775, the fort was the ruler's official residence until 1970 and

Ajman's police station in the 1970s. More appealing in some ways than its Dubai equivalent (the quieter, more parochial setting helps), and with a fine wind tower, which, unlike those in some other UAE museums, is fully functioning.

The museum showcases life in the region from ancient times to the modern era, with *barasti* houses and *dhows* just beyond the entrance and, in the old fort proper, displays on policing (practised since the days of the Prophet Mohammed in the 7th century), the bedroom of Sheikh Rashid Bin Humaid Al Nuaimi (1928–81) and a market tableau.

For a good stopping point in Ajman, try **Café Kranzler** (see ❹①).

### UMM AL QUWAIN

Continue through Ajman along Hamid Bin Abdul Aziz Street. At the first roundabout head for Al Ittihad Street at 11 o'clock. Carry on until this street joins Badr Street and turn left. You are now on the road to Umm Al Quwain. (If in doubt, follow signs for **Ras Al Khaimah**.) Follow this road for 26km (16 miles), at which point a sign pointing left to the side road to **Umm Al Quwain ❷**, a further 9km (5.5 miles) distant. After another 5km (3 miles) or so you reach Umm Al Quwain new town – little more than a rather bedraggled line of low-key shops flanking the main road, making it difficult to believe that you are actually in the capital of one of the seven

emitates. The whole place can be spookily quiet during the day – even in the old town you're likely to see more goats than people.

### The Old Town

On the far side of the modern town lies **Umm Al Quwain Old Town**, situated on its own sandy headland at the very end of the road. Three ancient watchtowers, once part of a fortified defensive wall, mark the boundary of the old town at the narrowest part of the headland, where King Faisal Road meets Al Soor Street. At this point you will see the old town away to your right across an enormous lagoon. On part of the lagoon's shoreline you will find one of Umm Al Quwain's most appealing attractions – a forest of mangrove trees.

### Umm Al Quwain Museum

Take the first right and follow the road past a small public park. The town's old fortress – which, like those elsewhere in the country, formerly served as the residence of the local ruler before being converted into a police station – stands in a small square beyond the roundabout ahead. This is now open to the public as the **Umm Al Quwain Museum** 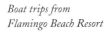 (Sat–Sun, Tue–Thur 8am–1pm and 5–8pm, Fri 5–8pm; charge). The restored fort itself offers a welcome contrast to the dusty streets outside, with its pretty coral stone buildings and a neat courtyard studded with trees. The museum is less appealing, with a decidedly dusty collection of traditional artefacts and some rather unexciting archeological finds (pots, mainly) from the nearby site of Ad-Dour *(see p.80)*.

### Boat trips from Flamingo Beach Resort

Take a right at the roundabout and follow Corniche Road past the fish market, where you are likely to see fishermen mending broken nets. Just before the road arcs left to continue

**Above:** strolling along the beach at Ajman.

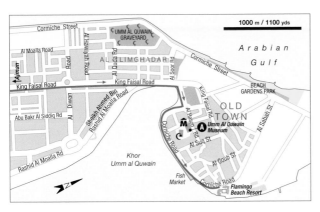

**Above:** a *dhow* against the sunset in Ras Al Khaimah.

its loop through the old town (before rejoining King Faisal Road), turn right into the low-key **Flamingo Beach Resort** (tel: 06 765 0000, www.flamingoresort.ae).

The resort offers various activities including boat trips, crab-hunting and deep-sea fishing expeditions (advance reservations essential). Boat trips (around Dhs200/hour) offer a nice way to see **As Siniyyah ❸** and the various other islands which dot the coast – the habitat of

---

## Aramaic Language

Aramaic lettering on coinage, bronze and stones at the archaeological site of Ad-Dour indicates that the language of Christ was the region's lingua franca in the pre-Islamic era, spread by dominant empires such as the Sassanids.

---

## Food and Drink

### ① CAFÉ KRANZLER
Ajman Kempinski Resort, Ajman; tel: 06 714 5555, www.kempinski.com; daily 24 hours; $$$
This terrace café-restaurant over-looking the gardens at the upmarket Kempinski Resort is nice for coffee or an early lunch, with tasty international fare including Asian, Middle Eastern and European dishes.

### ② LE CHALET
Al Hamra Fort Resort, Jazirat Al Hamra; tel: 07 244 6666; www.alhamrafort.com; daily 10am–10pm; $$$
Attractive beachfront restaurant overlooking the swimming pool terrace, offering well-prepared light meals, salads and seasonal specials.

### ③ AL BAHAR
Hilton Ras Al Khaimah Resort & Spa, on the northern side of RAK City, around 5km (3 miles) from the centre; tel: 07 228 8844; daily 11am–11pm; $$$
Laidback beachside restaurant serving up tasty barbecue lunches.

---

herons, cormorants, flamingos, turtles and even *dugong* (manatees or sea cows), which sailors of old mistook for mermaids *(see p.78)*.

### Ad-Dour Archaeological Site

Return to your car, retrace your steps back to the main Ras Al Khaimah highway and continue north for 8km (5 miles) to reach the low stone ruins of **Ad-Dour ❹**, an archaeological site to the right of the Ras Al Khaimah highway, opposite Khor Al Beidah. The largest pre-Islamic site on the Arabian Gulf, Ad-Dour (meaning 'the houses' in Arabic) was a major trading centre from around 300BC to AD100 and is a candidate for the great city of Omana, the Dubai of its day, which was known to classical geographers including Strabo and Pliny the Elder. Finds here have included Greek pottery and other artefacts, many of them on display in the Umm Al Quwain Museum *(see p.79)*.

### Dreamland Aqua Park

About 10km (6 miles) further along the highway a sign points off on the left to the **Dreamland Aqua Park ❺** (tel: 06 768 1888; www.dreamlanduae.com; daily Jan–Mar & Aug–Dec 10am–6pm; Apr–May Fri, Sat & Public Holidays until 7pm; June–July Fri & Public Holidays until 8pm; Ramadan 6pm–midnight; (NB: Fri, Sat & holidays strictly family days); charge), an unexpectedly large and well-equipped water park in this rather out-of-the-way location, including a huge wave pool, family raft rides and twister

slides – not as state-of-the-art as Wild Wadi and Aquaventure in Dubai, admittedly, but a fair bit cheaper and, during the week, a lot quieter as well.

*Al Hamra Fort Resort*

Another 13km (8 miles) up the road in the small town of Jazirat Al Hamra lies the impressive **Al Hamra Fort Resort** ❻ (tel: 07 244 6666, www.alhamrafort.com), designed in the form of a traditional Arabian fortress and occupying a prime slice of beachfront real estate. The resort is a good option for lunch, with a range of eating venues including **Le Chalet** (see ⑪②).

## RAS AL KHAIMAH

From here, it's just another 15km (9 miles) up the road to the regional capital of **Ras Al Khaimah** ❼ (usually abbreviated to 'RAK'), attractively backdropped by the distant red-rock mountains of the Musandam Peninsula further north in Oman. RAK is notably more built up and livelier than either Ajman or Umm Al Quwain, although much smaller compared to Dubai (or even Sharjah). The central souk area around the fort is worth a look for its traditional street life, usually busy with robed Emiratis and their wives, veiled from head to toe in black abayas – some still wear the traditional Bedu face masks which are much less common elsewhere in the country.

*Ras Al Khaimah National Museum*

The town's main attraction is, once again, its fort, now converted into the **Ras Al Khaimah National Museum** (Sat–Thur 8am–noon and 4–7pm, closed Fri; charge), a rather grand name for a decidedly modest museum which showcases the usual array of local artefacts and archeological finds, although the whole collection was being reorganised at the time of writing.

The 19th-century fort itself is the main attraction, with a fine wind tower looming over the shady courtyard within. For food, head to **Al Bahar** ⑪③ at the Hilton Ras Al Khaimah.

**Below:** an abra ride in calm water.

# AL AIN

*The attractive city of Al Ain – the UAE's largest inland settlement – offers a rewarding day-trip from Dubai, with a cluster of absorbing forts and souks, and one of the country's most beautiful oases.*

---

**DISTANCE** 270km
**TIME** A full day
**START/END** Dubai
**POINTS TO NOTE**

A car is essential to cover all of the sights in this itinerary, although the first section of the tour is eminently walkable, and gives a good taste of the city. If you don't want to drive, regular buses to Al Ain depart from Al Ghubaiba Bus Station in Bur Dubai (1hr 30min; Dhs20). Alternatively, many local tour operators run day trips covering many of the sights listed.

---

### Sheikh Zayed

Al Ain is particularly associated with the much-loved Sheikh Zayed Al Nahyan (ruled 1966–2004), ruler of Abu Dhabi and first president of the UAE, who oversaw the emirate's transformation from backwater Arabian village to global city-state. Zayed served as the ruler of Al Ain from 1946 until 1966, administering the area from his various forts and palaces in Al Ain and proving an unusually capable and charismatic ruler – British explorer Wilfred Thesiger was a particular admirer, and a regular guest at the sheikh's Al Jahili Fort.

### Al Ain National Museum and Sultan Zayed Fort

**Al Ain National Museum ❶** (Sat–Thur 8.30am–7.30pm, Fri 3–7.30pm, closed Mon; Dhs3; www.adach.ae) is a good starting point for tours of the city, with interesting displays covering local life and artefacts ranging from old Korans and antique silver jewellery through to photos of Abu Dhabi in the 1960s. **Sultan Bin Zayed Fort** (or Eastern Fort; same hours and ticket), next to the museum, is one of 20-odd forts in Al Ain and the surrounding desert. It's best known as the birthplace of Sheikh Zayed Bin Sultan Al Nahyan.

### Livestock Market and Al Ain Souk

Immediately behind the museum lies the city's **Livestock Market ❷**. It's busiest in the early morning, up to around 9am. Continue west to reach the bus station and the adjacent **Al Ain Souk ❸** (10am–10pm daily), the main meat, fruit and vegetable market, attracting various local characters.

### Al Ain Oasis

South of the souk stretches the idyllic **Al Ain Oasis ❹** (daily sunrise–sunset; free), the largest of the seven oases scattered across the city. Various entrances lead into the oasis, with a network of narrow walled lanes running between densely planted thickets of palm trees, dotted with fig and banana trees. The plantations are watered using the traditional *falaj* irrigation method, with mud-walled channels bringing water down from the surrounding mountains.

### Al Ain Palace Museum and Jahili Fort

Follow the road around the north side of the oasis behind the souk to reach the **Al Ain Palace Museum ❺** (Sat–Thur 8.30am–7.30pm, Fri 3–7.30pm; free). The sprawling complex has buildings set around courtyards and small gardens. Nearby stands the more interesting

**Jahili Fort** ❻ (Tue–Thur, Sat & Sun 9am–5pm, Fri 3–5pm; free), one of the finest traditional buildings in Al Ain, built in 1898. There is also an excellent exhibition showcasing the photographs and effects of explorer Wilfred Thesiger (1910–2003), who stayed at the fort in the late 1940s. Head north into the city centre and stop at **Al Mallah** (see ⑪①) for lunch or stay local at **Trader Vic's** (see ⑪②) in the Al Ain Rotana hotel.

## Camel Souk

The old-fashioned **Camel Souk** ❼ is also worth a visit, with its lively crowd haggling over the stock. The souk is busiest from 9–10am, although low-key trading may continue during the day. To reach the souk, take the road towards Mazyad from the roundabout in front of the Hilton hotel. After about three km (2 miles) you'll see Bawadi mall on your left; the souk is past this, on the left.

### Food and Drink 🍴

**① AL MALLAH**
Just south of Globe Roundabout, northern edge of Al Ain city centre; daily 10am–midnight; $
A popular Lebanese café, good for inexpensive but tasty fare, including shwarmas and juices. No alcohol.

**② TRADER VIC'S**
Al Ain Rotana; tel: 03 754 5111; daily 12.30–3.30pm and 7.30–11.30pm; $$$
Al Ain branch of the popular Polynesian-themed chain serving up cheery (if rather overpriced) international food backed up by some of the UAE's most potent cocktails.

## Hili Gardens

On the northern side of the city, the **Hili Gardens and Archaeological Park** ❽ (daily 9am–10pm; Dhs1) is one of the most important archaeological sites in the UAE. The Great Hili Tomb, dating from the 3rd century BC, is decorated with primitive carvings.

## Jebel Hafeet

Some 30km south of Al Ain on the Omani border rises **Jebel Hafeet** ❾ (1,180m/3,870ft), the second highest mountain in the UAE. It's about a half-hour drive, with glorious views; the terrace at the Mercure Grand hotel, just below the summit, makes a memorable – if surprisingly chilly – spot for a drink.

### Over the border to Buraimi
The border with Oman lies about 1km (0.6 miles) north of central Al Ain, beyond which stretches the adjoining Omani city of Buraimi, where you'll find the old forts of Al Khandaq and Al Hillah, along with a lively souk. Foreign tourists wanting to cross into Oman can travel via the border post north of Al Ain at Hili. Outside weekends and holidays it should take under 30 minutes and costs around $40 in visa fees.

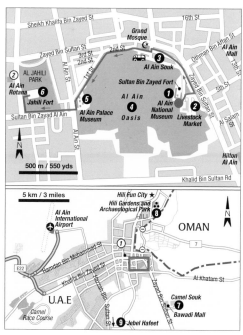

# FUJAIRAH AND THE EAST COAST

*The emirate of Fujairah, straddling the eastern coast of the UAE, offers a rewarding escape from the busy city, with wild mountains, deserted beaches and a pleasantly somnolent pace of life.*

**Snoopy Island**

Just offshore from Fujairah's Sandy Beach Motel lies the rocky outcrop popularly known as 'Snoopy Island' on account of its supposed resemblance to the lovable beagle in the *Peanuts* comic strip by Charles Schulz.

---

**DISTANCE** 212km (132 miles) round trip

**TIME** A full day

**START/END** Dubai

**POINTS TO NOTE**

A rental car *(see p.106)* is required for this tour, although if you don't fancy driving, many tour operators in Dubai offer 'east coast' tours which cover most or all of the places below.

---

Hugging the eastern coast of the UAE, the beautiful emirate of Fujairah offers a striking contrast to Dubai, its craggy coastline, deserted beaches and dramatic **wadis** barely touched by tourism. The emirate is categorised by its string of quiet towns dotting the coast, backed by the rocky Hajar mountains, and secluded and largely deserted beaches between. The beach resorts of Al Aqah are a popular weekend retreat for Dubai expats,

## EAST TO MASAFI

From Dubai, it's a two-hour drive to Al Aqah, on the coast north of Fujairah city. For the first part of the journey,

take the E311 Emirates Road towards Sharjah International Airport, then follow the signs to Al Dhaid.

At Junction 8 of the Sharjah-Al Dhaid road you pass **Sharjah Desert Park ❶** (tel: 06 531 1411; www.sharjah tourism.ae/en; Sat, Mon–Wed 9am–7pm, Thur noon–7pm, Fri 2–10pm; charge). Set up in 1995, the park houses an interesting natural history museum and botanical museum, while the attached wildlife centre serves as a breeding ground for rare Arabian leopards, foxes, ibex, oryx and gazelles.

At Al Dhaid, a small oasis town that is kept green by ancient *falaj* channels fed by mountain springs, follow the signs to Masafi and Fujairah.

## MASAFI

The scenery now starts to change from plains to mountains. In a small gorge about 5km (3 miles) before reaching the modest little town of **Masafi ❷**, perhaps best known as the source of the popular brand of UAE mineral water. The town is also home to a lively 'Friday Market' (actually open all week, despite its name). This consists of a long string of shops lining the main road

through town, selling various souvenirs and handicrafts including ornamental pots and huge quantities of carpets, although most are machine-made, and of low quality.

Head left at the large roundabout in the centre of Masafi, following the signs for Dibba and Al Aqah. From here the road rises and falls through striking mountain scenery before passing south of Dibba town.

## DIBBA

Nestled below the mountains at the southern end of the Musandam Peninsula and at the tip of the Arabian peninsula, **Dibba ❸** is actually three towns in one. The largest part of town, known as Dibba Muhallab, belongs to the emirate of Fujairah. Next to this is the smaller area known as Dibba Al Hisn, administered by the emirate of Sharjah, and Dibba Bayah, over the border in Oman.

Though isolated, this area has a rich history: in 633AD the Muslim forces of Caliph Abu Baker waged a great battle on this spot to suppress a local rebellion and claim the Arabian peninsula for Islam. The site of the battle is now marked by an enormous cemetery containing some 10,000 stones marking the graves of those who lost their lives.

### Dibba Muhallab and into Oman

Dibba Muhallab itself is one of the more pleasant towns in the UAE, although there's not much to see from

**Above from far left:**
An example of the charming coastline along the eastern coast; traditional pottery.

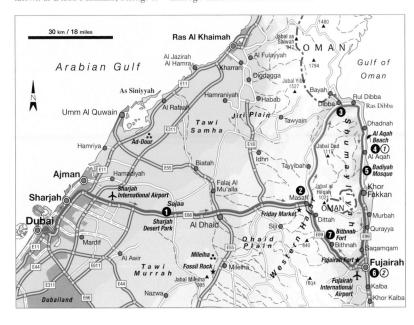

**Fujairah Coastline**
Fujairah is the only emirate located entirely along the Gulf of Oman (Arabian Sea), with 90km (56 miles) of coastline.

a tourist point of view apart from a couple of huge mosques, each sporting a quartet of minarets, on the seafront corniche, and the quirky sequence of oversized sculptures which adorn the town's various roundabouts (including a monster coffeepot, oil lamp and a pile of earthenware pottery).

From here, it's possible to make a pleasant side trip over the border to Dibba Bayah and dip your toe into Oman (no visa required, although you'll have to show your passport). The town itself is pleasantly sleepy, fringed with a fine swathe of sand and dotted with fishing boats, often with considerable quantities of fish laid out to dry on the sand. Just inland (signposted as 'Daba Castle') lies the town's impressive fort – a fine example of traditional Omani architecture, though it isn't open to the public.

*Al Aqah Beach*
Back in the car, retrace your route through Dibba and head south, following the signs to Fujairah. After around 15km (9 miles) you will reach the idyllic **Al Aqah Beach** ❹, now home to a trio of upmarket resort hotels which attract hordes of visiting Dubaians during the weekend (although things are pretty quiet during the week). The major landmark here is towering **Le Meridien Al Aqah** resort (tel: 09 244 9000, www.lemeridien-alaqah.com), an incongruously grand structure which looks like it's been airlifted straight from Dubai Marina. Just down the road stands the equally vast **Fujairah Rotana** (tel: 09 244 9888; www.rotana.com) and, a short distance further on, the more homely **Sandy Beach Motel** (tel: 09 244 5555; www.sandybm.com). All three offer an appealing spot to hole up for a night or two, enjoying the find wide sands and swimming and snorkelling in the unspoilt coastal waters. All offer a range of places to grab some lunch, including the attractive **The Views** at the Meridien Al Aqah resort (see ⑪①).

## BADIYAH AND KHOR FAKKAN

Continuing along the coast towards Fujairah city, it's around 8km (5 miles) to the historic 15th-century **Badiyah Mosque** ❺ (daily 24hrs; free), the oldest mosque in the UAE, on the right of the road. Non-Muslims may be permitted inside outside prayer time for a glimpse of the atmospheric interior, while there are stunning views of the sea and mountains from the watchtower on the hill above.

## Food and Drink 🍴

**① THE VIEWS**
Le Meridien Al Aqah Beach Resort, Al Aqah; tel: 09 244 9000, www.lemeridien-alaqah.com; open 24hr; $$$
A pleasant lunch stop, with fine sea views and international food from the brasserie-style menu.

**② NEPTUNIA**
Hilton Fujairah Resort, Fujairah City; tel: 09 222 2411; daily noon–midnight; $$$
Pleasant spot for lunch or an early dinner before heading back to Dubai, with sea views and a mainly Mediterranean and Arabian menu.

A further 10km (6 miles) down the road, the small port the **Khor Fakkan** (actually part of the emirate of Sharjah) is the next major town along the coast, with a seafront corniche spread along a handsome stretch of coast.

## FUJAIRAH CITY

Even the low-key high-rises and modest urban sprawl of **Fujairah City** ❻ can come as something of a surprise after the undeveloped countryside further up the oast. Most of the city's new-found wealth is thanks to its huge port, from which most of the UAE's oil is exported – long lines of tankers can usually be seen queueing offshore.

Oil apart, the main attraction in the city is the fine **Fujairah Fort** (tel: 09 222 9085; Sun–Thur 8.30am–5pm, Fri 2–5pm; charge), on the Masafi side of the city. Dating back 500 years in places, this is the oldest fort in the UAE and perhaps the most impressive, set against a stunning mountain backdrop. If you want something to eat before turning back to Dubai, head for the attractive **Neptunia** restaurant at the Hilton Fujairah (see ⑪②).

### Bithnah Fort

From Fujairah, follow the signs back to Masafi. Some 15km (9 miles) from Fujairah City, the quiet village of Bithnah is home to the atmospheric old **Bithnah Fort** ❼ into the right of the highway as it twists and turns through the mountains, set above the village's sprawling oasis (but not open to the public).

### Bullfighting

Traditional Arab sports such as falconry and camel racing are not suited to the terrain of the east coast. As a result, the large Brahmin bull, which has worked for centuries in the area's palm groves, is bred to compete. The contest is between two large, pampered bulls, each weighing a tonne (ton) or more and fed on a diet of milk, honey and meal. The bulls try to force each other to the ground. Winners are also declared if an opposing bull turns and flees. The sport was possibly introduced in the 16th century by the Portuguese, although it may also pre-date Islam with its source in Persia, where the bull was once worshipped. The Fujairah contests are held on weekends in winter, near the palm groves off the Kalba/Oman road.

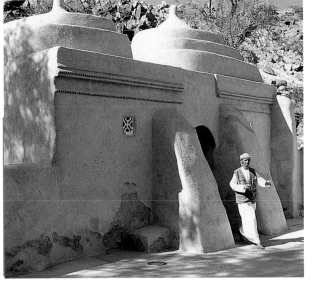

# ABU DHABI

*The wealthier and more sedate capital of the UAE is an interesting contrast to its glitzy neighbour, Dubai. Abu Dhabi doesn't disappoint, however, and you'll find it has its own fair share of beautiful beaches, swanky hotels and a couple of the country's landmark attractions.*

**Above:** Al Maqta Bridge; tower of Al Hosn Palace.

**'Father of the Gazelle'**
Abu Dhabi means 'Father of the Gazelle'. According to local lore, the city was founded in 1793 after Bedu hunters from the Bani Yas tribe in the desert interior chased a gazelle to the coast. Chancing upon a freshwater spring, they saw the area was habitable and finally settled here.

**DISTANCE** 238km (147 miles) round trip
**TIME** A full day
**START/END** Abu Dhabi
**POINTS TO NOTE**
Regular buses to Abu Dhabi depart from Al Ghubaiba Bus Station in Bur Dubai every 30 minutes between 5.30am and 11.30pm (Dhs20 one way), although given that the journey can take around two hours or longer, this makes for a very long day trip. Taxis are a more expensive option (Dhs250 one way). Ideally, it's worth renting a car, which will get you to Abu Dhabi much quicker than the bus and will also allow you to get around the various sights (which are widely spread out) without constantly jumping in and out of cabs. The drive is straightforward and quick (around 1hr 30mins each way) – follow the Abu Dhabi signs along Sheikh Zayed Road (E11).

In the past Abu Dhabi, the federal capital of the UAE, has had a rather cool approach to tourism, and tourists have been equally cool in return. With more than 94 percent of the UAE's oil reserves (some 10 percent of the world's total), the emirate hasn't needed to diversify its economy and rely on tourism in the way that Dubai has. The city is slowly waking up to the benefits of tourism, however, with a string of ongoing mega-developments aimed at raising its global profile.

Located on an island, Abu Dhabi is accessed via the Al Maqta Bridge. The old watchtower, which is visible from the bridge, can be seen in early black-and-white photographs of the city, when camel trains crossed from the mainland to the island at low tide.

## AL HOSN PALACE AND CULTURAL FOUNDATION

The historic heart of the city is the **Al Hosn Palace ❶** or 'White Fort' (currently closed for renovation), Abu Dhabi's oldest building, located on Khaled Bin Al Waleed Street, a couple of blocks from the corniche at the top of the island. Built in 1793, the year the city was established, it was the residence of the ruling Al Nahyan family before finally becoming a visitor attraction. The original fort was built to protect the town's well, and the outer walls and tower were added at a later date. Today, its ancient battlements stand in stark contrast to the high-rise offices, apartments and hotels that surround it.

Next door to Al Hosn stands the attractive modern **Abu Dhabi Cultural Foundation ②**, the only arts centre of its kind in the region – although, like Al Hosn, it's currently closed whilst the area is redeveloped. This centre was set up under the patronage of Sheikh Zayed and runs a busy programme of artistic events, including the Emirates Film Festival and an international book fair. The ever-popular **Lebanese Flower** restaurant (see ⑪①) is close to Al Hosn, and a great place to stop for lunch.

### THE CORNICHE

A short walk along Khaled Bin Al Waleed Street leads to the 8km (5-mile) -long corniche, the longest in the UAE. The best time to visit is late afternoon (or Fridays and weekends in the winter), when the population of Abu Dhabi seems to head down here to stroll or jog through the breezy gardens lining the waterfront. The several nearby parks are packed with kite-flyers on Fridays and public holidays.

*Emirates Palace Hotel*

To the west, the corniche continues towards the presidential palace and the landmark **Emirates Palace Hotel ③**, one of the most opulent in the world. Constructed in traditional Arabian style, this red-sandstone collosus sprawls for the best part of a kilometre (0.6 miles) down the beach, topped

**Above from far left:** Al Hosn Palace; heading for the shops; desert sunset; interior of the Emirates Palace Hotel.

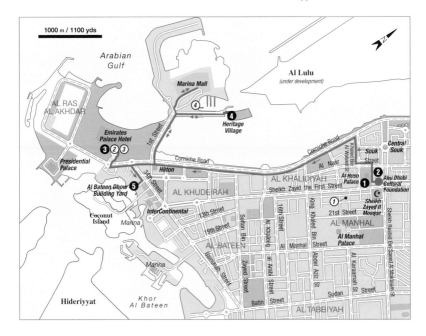

## Saadiyat Island

Foremost amongst Abu Dhabi's planned mega-projects is the massive new Saadiyat Island Cultural District, located on Saadiyat Island, around 3km (2 miles) from the city centre and due to start opening from 2014 onwards (although estimated completion dates are being constantly set back). The island will feature an unprecedented number of institutions by world-famous architects, including a branch of the Guggenheim museum designed by Frank Gehry (who also designed the iconic Guggenheim in Bilbao), the Louvre Abu Dhabi by French architect Jean Nouvel, a performing arts centre by Iraqi architect Zaha Hadid, a maritime museum by Japanese architect Tadao Ando and a national museum by British architect Norman Foster.

with around a hundred domes, while the interior is a riot of Arabian chintz, best appreciated over afternoon tea in the foyer (see ⑪②). It's also a great place to enjoy an upmarket dinner – **Mezzaluna** (see ⑪③) is good, and not too pricey.

On the Breakwater near Marina Mall is the 1,600 sq m (17,223 sq ft) **Heritage Village** ❹ (tel: 02 681 4455; Sat–Thur 9am–5pm, Fri 3.30–9pm; free), which illustrates the history of the emirate before oil revenues transformed the landscape. There is an exhibition of Bedouin tents, a reconstruction of a palm house, old fishing villages and traditional souks. In addition, it offers a fabulous view of the Abu Dhabi skyline across the water. The **Havana Café**, see ⑪④, is nearby.

*Al Bateen Dhow Yard*

Located on the other side of the Emirates Palace Hotel from the Breakwater, close to the Inter Continental Hotel on the west of the island, **Al Bateen Dhow Building Yard** ❺ is one of the few surviving traditional boatyards in the UAE. Visitors are welcome to wander around; piles of teak planks lie ready to be shaped into wooden sailing *dhows*, a sight that has changed very little over the centuries.

### THE OUTSKIRTS

Two of Abu Dhabi's biggest modern landmarks lie on the edge of the city, a contrasting pair of attractions showcasing the emirate's religious fervour with its more recent obsession with cars.

### Food and Drink

**① LEBANESE FLOWER**
Off 26th Street, near Al Hosn; $$
An Abu Dhabi institution, tucked away in a side street near Al Hosn, this Lebanese restaurant is the best place in the city to fill up on inexpensive Middle Eastern food, with an excellent selection of grills, kebabs and mezze.

**② EMIRATES PALACE CAFÉ**
Emirates Palace, Corniche West Street; tel: 02 690 7999; daily 6.30am–1am; $$$
The café in the foyer of the opulent Emirates Palace Hotel provides a sumptuous setting for a memorable – if expensive – high tea, served in the lobby level café from 4–7pm daily.

**③ MEZZALUNA**
Emirates Palace hotel 02 690 7999; daily 12.30–3pm and 7–11pm; $$$$
This is the place to come for a slice of opulence (and it is less expensive than other restaurants in the hotel), with superb traditional Italian and Mediterranean dishes.

**④ HAVANA CAFÉ**
Near Marina Mall, Breakwater; tel: 02 681 0044; daily 9am–2am; $$
The mainly Arabic menu also includes international fare such as sandwiches and pizza. Patio and rooftop seating are available in the cooler months, with excellent views across the Abu Dhabi waterfront to the high rises along the Corniche.

### Sheikh Zayed Grand Mosque

Some 10km from the city centre, close to Al Maqta Bridge, the monumental **Sheikh Zayed Grand Mosque** ❻ (Sat–Thur 9am–9pm, Fri 4–9pm; interior closed for about 30min during prayers at 12.30pm, 3.30pm, 6pm & 7.30pm; free; free guided tours Sat–Thur at 10am) rises imperiously over the city. This is undoubtedly Abu Dhabi's single most worthwhile attraction: a spectacular, snow-white mass of domes and minarets visible for miles around – the vast courtyard alone is capable of accommodating some 40,000 worshippers. Completed in 2007, the mosque is one of the world's biggest – and certainly the most expensive, having cost some $500 million. It's also one of only two mosques in the UAE (along with the Jumeira Mosque in Dubai; *see p.56*) open to non-Muslims. If visiting, you'll be expected to dress conservatively; female visitors not suitably attired will be offered a black abaya to wear.

### Yas Island

Some 20km from the city centre, off the Dubai highway, Yas Island is home to the city's new Formula 1 racetrack (which has staged the final race in the F1 season since 2010) and the state-of-the-art new **Ferrari World Abu Dhabi** theme park ❼ (Tue–Sun noon–10pm; entrance charge), featuring over 20 rides and attractions, including the world's fastest rollercoaster and F1 racing simulators, plus plenty more sedate family rides and kids' attractions, and a driving school.

**Above from far left:** local boy and horse; scaling a palm tree; romantic moment on the beach; along the Corniche.

### Sports Events

Abu Dhabi already has a world-class sporting event in the form of the European Tour-sanctioned Abu Dhabi Golf Championship, held at Abu Dhabi Golf Club in January. Among the big names to play here are Retief Goosen, Padraig Harrington, Sergio Garcia and Henrik Stenson.

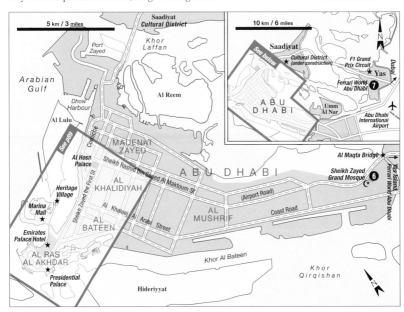

# DIRECTORY

A user-friendly alphabetical listing of practical information,
plus hand-picked hotels and restaurants, clearly organised
by area, to suit all budgets and tastes.

# A

## AGE RESTRICTIONS

Car rental agencies require drivers to be at least 21 or 22 years old. This rises to 25 and 30 depending on the vehicle category. Children under 10 are not allowed to sit in the front passenger seat of cars. Entry to bars and nightclubs varies between 18 and 21. On the water and in theme parks, the minimum age for some activities is seven or eight, but it also depends on the height of the child (often with a minimum of 1.2m/4ft). For diving lessons, the minimum age for junior open water training is 10, but kids can begin learning in a pool from the age of eight.

## ALCOHOL

Unless you're a Dubai resident with an alcohol licence, you may only buy alcohol for consumption in hotel bars, restaurants and clubs, and in a very small number of mall restaurants. Drinking alcohol in public, outside licensed venues, is strictly illegal.

# B

## BUDGETING

Dubai is an expensive city to visit. Accommodation is probably the main expense, while fancier restaurants and alcohol all come at a considerable price. On the plus side, it's possible to eat well and cheaply at many places around the city, while public transport, either on the city's metro or in taxis, is also good value for money.

**Accommodation**: The cost for a standard double room ranges from around Dhs350 per night in a one-star city centre hotel to Dhs575–1,000 at a four-star hotel, and Dhs1,000–3,500 at a five-star hotel.

**Eating and Drinking**: It is possible to pick up a filling sandwich in a street-level Lebanese restaurant or a curry in a no-nonsense Indian or Pakistani outlet for as little as Dhs15. Main courses in most decent Western-style, non-hotel restaurants are between Dhs25–45. For fine dining, budget upwards of Dhs55 per person for mains. For a three-course dinner for two with wine at a five-star hotel venue, budget for upwards of Dhs600.

Cans of soft drinks start at Dhs1 in shops, but are heavily marked up in restaurants. Freshly made juices cost between Dhs6–15. Alcoholic drinks are generally more expensive than they would be in the West.

**Transport**: Package deals arranged from your home country are likely to be cheaper than separately arranged air travel and accommodation. The best prices are found in low season (July–September), but that's because it is the hottest time of the year in the UAE.

Generally taxis are cheaper than those in Western cities, although the

Above from far
left: shadows
of children on
horseback; arid
desert climate.

taxi fare from the airport comes with a Dhs20 mark-up. A creek crossing on an *abra* (water taxi) is just Dhs1, while fares on the city's metro and buses are also just a few dirhams.

## C

### CHILDREN

Childcare facilities are on a par with those in the West. Most malls have changing facilities in the women's public toilets; many also have supervised indoor play areas.

### CLIMATE

Summers are very hot and humid. From May to September, daytime temperatures are rarely below 40°C (104°F) with humidity up to 90 per cent. From October to April the weather resembles that of an exceptionally good European summer, with temperatures hovering around 30°C (mid-80s°F) and little or no humidity.

Evenings can feel a little chilly around January and February, so jumpers may be required. Annual rainfall is minimal (an average of 42mm/1½in), but downpours occur from January to March – and when it rains, it pours. Inland, Hatta is a little cooler, particularly at night in winter.

### CLOTHING

Comfortable loose cottons suit the climate best, with peak caps or sun hats for optimum protection during the heat of the day. In terms of culture, while the most daring swimwear is acceptable on the beach, around town visitors should be more modest and avoid wearing very short shorts and dresses, and tight tops. Outside Dubai, more care should be taken to avoid showing too much bare skin: upper arms should be covered, and women are advised to wear long skirts or trousers. Winter evenings can be surprisingly cool, so pack a cardigan or jumper.

### CRIME AND SAFETY

Dubai is a relatively safe city. Both petty theft and major crimes are rare and the level of personal security is high. Many women feel comfortable on their own in the evening. However, while you can let your guard down to some extent, it is best to avoid complacency; take the same precautions you would take anywhere else.

Tourists typically find themselves in trouble with the law because they are unaware of, or have disregarded UAE laws regarding alcohol, drugs and public displays of affection. Drunken or disorderly behaviour (including swearing) could land you a spell in prison. It is important to note that some medication (such as codeine and temazepam), available over the counter in other parts of the world, are illegal in the UAE. Check with your health practitioner before entering the country. The UAE also practises zero tolerance to drugs and drink driving *(see p.14 and 160)*.

The US-led 'war on terror' has

**Bookstores**
Easily the best
bookstore in Dubai
is the superb
Kinokuniya in the
Dubai Mall.
Borders, in Mall of
the Emirates, is also
good, while there
are branches of
local chain
Magrudy's in most
malls; their original
branch in Jumeira
(near the mosque)
is particularly good.

caused increased concerns for the safety of citizens of countries associated with military activity in the region. The UAE is no exception and vigilance against terrorism is recommended. However, there have been no incidents, the country is an ally of the US, and Emiratis are generally friendly to Westerners.

Dubai Police has a Tourist Security Department, tel: 800 4438.

## CUSTOMS

The duty-free allowances entering the UAE are as follows: 400 cigarettes, 50 cigars or 0.5kg (1lb) loose tobacco, and – for non-Muslims – four litres of alcohol (or 12 cans of beer). There are no limits on perfume.

## D

## DISABLED TRAVELLERS

Dubai is one the Middle East's most accessible destinations. Most of the city's more upmarket hotels now have specially adapted rooms for disabled travellers, as do some of the city's malls, including disabled parking spaces and specially equipped toilets. Transport is also fairly well-equipped. Dubai Taxi (tel: 04 208 0808) has specially designed vehicles equipped with ramps and lifts, while the Dubai Metro features tactile guide paths, lifts and ramps to assist visually- and mobility-impaired visitors, as well as wheelchair spaces in all compartments,. The city's water

buses can also be used by mobility-impaired visitors, and staff will assist you in boarding and disembarking. There are also dedicated facilities for passengers with special needs at the airport. Sadly, most of the city's older heritage buildings are not accessible (with the exception of the Dubai Museum).

## E

## ELECTRICITY

Voltage in Dubai is 220/240 volts, 50 cycles AC. British-style three-pin sockets are common; if needed, adaptors can be bought from electrical shops all over the city.

## EMBASSIES

**Australia**: BurJuman Centre; tel: 04 508 7100; www.dfat.gov.au/missions.
**Canada**: 7th floor, Bank Street Building, Bur Dubai; tel: 04 314 5555; www.dfait-maeci.gc.ca.
**France**: API World Tower, Sheikh Zayed Road; tel: 04 332 9040; www.ambafrance-eau.org.
**Ireland**: Riyadh, Kingdom of Saudi Arabia; tel: +966 1 488 2300; www.embassyofireland-riyadh.com.
**New Zealand**: Riyadh, Kingdom of Saudi Arabia; tel: +966 1 488 7988; www.mfat.govt.nz.
**South Africa**: Villa Number 202, corner of Airport Road and 25th Street, Abu Dhabi; tel: 02 447 3446.
**UK**: Al Seef Road, Bur Dubai; tel: 04 309 4444; www.britishembassy.gov.uk.

**US**: 21st Floor, Dubai World Trade
Centre, Sheikh Zayed Road;
tel: 04 311 6000; http://dubai.us
consulate. gov.

## EMERGENCIES

As in the UK, the emergency number
to call for the police or an ambulance
is 999; the fire service is on 997. For
Dubai Police's Tourist Security
Department, dial 800 4438.

## ETIQUETTE

Dubai is one of the more liberal
Gulf cities, and nationals are both
familiar with and reasonably tolerant
of those from other cultures. Even
so, any extra effort to respect Arab
sensibilities is greatly appreciated.

Do not try and rush things, particularly with officialdom, which likes
to take its time even over matters of
apparent urgency – patience is a
virtue; don't photograph men without first asking their permission and
never photograph or even stare at
local women; don't offer alcohol to
Muslims; don't show the soles of
your feet when sitting among locals;
don't eat, drink or smoke in public
areas during the holy month of
Ramadan – the penalties are severe;
and never drink and drive – you
could end up in jail for a month.

Away from the beach, dress modestly, and if time permits, do gra-
ciously accept any hospitality that's
offered – a refusal would be considered rude.

# F

## FESTIVALS

**January–February**: Dubai Shopping
Festival (DSF), a month-long, city-
wide festival with discounts at partici-
pating outlets. The festival also
includes heritage and entertainment
events, funfairs and pyrotechnic shows
daily on the Creek, and the popular
Global Village (www.globalvillage.ae)
in Dubailand, with colourful pavilions
showcasing arts and crafts from countries around the world.

**February**: The three-day Dubai
International Jazz Festival is held at
an open-air venue at Dubai Media
City. It regularly attracts some of the
best jazz performers in the world.
(www.dubaijazzfest.com).

**July–August**: A summer version of
DSF *(see above)*, the Dubai Summer
Surprises (DSS) is another retail hap-
pening with most events tending to
be held in malls. (www.mydsf.com).

**November**: The Dubai Airshow is a
biennial extravaganza of a trade event
that is closed to the public. From the
streets around Dubai International
Airport, however, you can see the
afternoon flying displays by forma-
tion teams such as Britain's Red
Arrows. The gala dinner is invitation-
only, but the post-dinner concert by a
big-name international star is open to
the public. For more details, see
www.dubaiairshow.org.

**December**: National Day is a three-day holiday in the first week of December that marks the founding of the UAE in 1971. Parks and public places host cultural activities such as folk dancing, and at night the city is festooned in lights.

The Dubai International Film Festival (DIFF), which was inaugurated in 2004, attracts film-makers and stars from Hollywood, Bollywood and the Middle East. The red-carpet events and most screenings, which members of the public can buy tickets for, are held at Madinat Jumeirah. (www.dubaifilmfest.com).

## FURTHER READING

*Arabia* by Jonathan Raban. Classic account of the modern Gulf states, first published in 1979, and offering a fascinating record of the region during a period of immense change.

*Arabian Destiny* by Edward Henderson, (Motivate, 1999). The memoirs of a long-term UAE resident and a gripping account of the country's evolution.

*Dubai: the Story of the World's Fastest City* (published in North America as City of Gold: *Dubai and the Dream of Capitalism*) by Jim Krane. Superb introduction to the city, with absorbing coverage of Dubai's history and what makes the modern metropolis tick.

*Dubai: the Vulnerability of Success,* by Christopher M. Davidson. Detailed scholarly study of the history of Dubai, plus chapters on the city's social, political and economic workings.

# G

## GAY AND LESBIAN

Homosexuality is not tolerated in the UAE and is officially illegal, so discretion is strongly advised.

# H

## HEALTH

**Hygiene/General Health**: Dubai is a modern, reasonably clean city. Its public lavatories are well maintained (the WCs are almost all Western-style), and it is safe to drink the tap water, though most residents prefer to drink bottled water, which is advisable anyway outside of Dubai. One of the most popular brands of bottled water is the locally produced Masafi.

Due to widespread construction work, the air in Dubai is very dusty, so people who battle with asthma or their sinuses might suffer.

**Medical/Dental Services**: Healthcare is of a high standard in Dubai, but expensive, so it is wise to take out travel insurance. There are good government hospitals as well as numerous private clinics. The main emergency hospital is the government-run Rashid Hospital (tel: 04 337 4000) near Maktoum Bridge in Bur Dubai; emergency treatment is free here. A consul-

tation with a doctor in non-emergency cases costs around Dhs100.

For emergencies with children, Al Wasl Hospital (tel: 04 324 1111), across the highway from Wafi City, is a renowned paediatric hospital.

Dental problems can be dealt with by the American Dental Clinic (tel: 04 344 0668, www.american-dental-clinic.com) or the Swedish Dental Clinic (tel: 04 223 1297, www.swedish dentalclinic.net).

**Pharmacies**: There are useful branches of the BinSina chain, open 24 hours, at various locations around the city including Mankhool Road in Bur Dubai just north of the Ramada hotel; on the Creek side of Baniyas Square (just east of the Deira Tower); in southern Jumeirah by the turn-off to the Majlis Ghorfat Um Al Sheif; and in Satwa on Al Diyafah Street near the Al Mallah restaurant.

**Vaccinations**: No special inoculations are required prior to visiting the UAE.

## HOURS AND HOLIDAYS

**Business Hours**: Dubai runs on an Islamic calendar, with the weekend falling on Friday and Saturday. Government offices work from 7 or 7.30am–1.30pm Sun–Thur. International companies keep the hours of 9am–5pm Sun–Thur. Local companies and shops typically open 9/10am–1/1.30pm and 4/4.30–9/10pm Sat–Thur. Generally, banks are open 8am–1pm Sat–Thur; some also open Fri 8am–noon. Larger shopping malls open from 10am–10pm Sat–Thur and on Fri from around 2pm–late evening.

**Public Holidays**: Religious holidays are governed by the Islamic *(Hegira)* calendar and therefore do not fall on fixed dates. The main holidays are as follows: *Eid Al Fitr* (the end of Ramadan); *Eid Al Adha* (during the month of the *Haj*, or pilgrimage to Mecca); the ascension of the Prophet; the Prophet's birthday; and Islamic New Year. Check with the Ministry of Information and Culture: www.uaeinteract.com, for dates. Other public holidays are New Year's Day (1 January) and National Day (2 December).

## INSURANCE

Visitors should take out the standard policies that cover loss of property and emergency medical care.

## INTERNET

Access to certain websites may be blocked due to political, religious or sexual content. Internet connectivity is available in the guest rooms and business centres of larger hotels, although often at exorbitant rates. Internet cafés are surprisingly thin on the ground except for in Bur Dubai (where they can be found in many of the small roads and alleyways off Al Fahidi Street). One reliable place is the Al Jalssa internet café (Dhs10/hr; daily

Health Requirements
Do note that an immunisation certificate for cholera and yellow fever will be required if you are arriving from an infected area, such as parts of Africa and South America.

8am–midnight) in the Al Ain centre. Elsewhere, the Grano Coffee shop in Wafi (Dhs14/hr) is one of the few reliable places.

Things are a lot easier if you have your own WiFi-enabled laptop and can access one of the numerous free WiFi hotspots around the city, including the whole of the Dubai Mall. You can also get online on the Dubai Metro for Dhs10 hr. Various WiFi hotspots are also operated by the city's two telecom companies, Eitsalat (www.etisalat.ae) and Du (www.du.ae), which offer access at numerous places around the city, including most of the city's malls and numerous coffee shops, with various pay-as-you-go packages. See the websites for full details of charges and hotspot locations.

## L

## LANGUAGE

The official language is Arabic, but English is widely spoken and understood. It's unlikely that you'll encounter any difficulty using English in hotels, restaurants and shopping malls, but it could be useful to learn a few words and phrases in Arabic:

hello *marhaba*
welcome *ahlan wa-sahlan (ahlan)*
peace be with you (greeting)
*as-salaam alaykum*
and with you be peace (response)
*wa-alaykum as-salaam*
good morning *sabah al khayr*
good morning (response)
*sabah al nour*
good evening *masaa al khayr*
good evening (response) *masaa al nour*
my name is… *ana ismi…*
what is your name? *shou ismac?*
how are you? *kayf haalak?*
well *zein*
you're welcome *afwan*
please *min fadlak*
thank you *shukran*
yes *naam*
no *la*
goodbye, peace be with you
*maa as-salaama*

## LEFT LUGGAGE

The left luggage facility at Dubai International Airport is located in Arrivals (tel: 04 216 1734). At time of printing the cost for a normal size case was Dhs10 for 12 hours. Other options for left luggage are limited to the hotel you have been staying in, which should be willing to hold your luggage for a few hours after you have checked out.

## LOST PROPERTY

There are many stories of lost property being returned. The key is to follow up with the relevant authority or organisation in the general area where your property may have been lost. This might include a local police station, mall management office, taxi company, hotel or bar. It's always worth putting in a call. The number for lost property (Baggage Services) at Dubai International Airport is 04 224 5383 or email them via the lost and found form

Above from far
left: Dubai signs;
modern blocks.

at www.dubaiairport.com. If you leave something in a taxi or on the metro, call the RTA on 04 800 9090.

# M

## MEDIA

**Newspapers**: Dubai press is heavily censored and local journalists usually steer well clear of expressing negative or controversial opinions about local matters, making for a rather dull media. International magazines commonly have any offending material (nude women, for example) masked with black marker. Local English-language newspapers are the broadsheet *Gulf News*, *Khaleej Times*, *The Gulf Today*, and the tabloids *Emirates Today* and *7 Days*, although easily the best local paper is *The National*, published in Abu Dhabi, but with extensive coverage of events in Dubai. Foreign newspapers and English-language publications such as the *International Herald Tribune*, *USA Today* and *Weekly Telegraph* can be found in supermarkets. Most British newspapers arrive a day late, with the exception of *The Times* and *The Sunday Times*, which are printed in Dubai. The main sources of information on events are *Time Out Dubai* and *What's On* magazines.

**Radio**: The city has a couple of local English-language radio stations, including Virgin Radio Dubai (104.4 FM; virginradiodubai.com) and

Dubai 92 (92FM; dubai92.com), churning out mainstream western pop and inane chat.

**Television**: Dubai's English-language TV station is the government-run Dubai One, which broadcasts Western movies and TV programmes, but has a local English-language news programme, Emirates News, at 8.30pm daily. Hotels also offer satellite and cable television with international news channels such as CNN and Sky.

## MONEY

**Cash Machines**: There are globally linked ATM points at banks, malls and some hotels.

**Credit Cards**: Major cards such as Visa, MasterCard, American Express and Diners Club are widely accepted in hotels, restaurants and shops. But if you plan to bargain, it's better to have cash.

**Currency**: The UAE dirham (abbreviated to Dhs, dh or AED). One dirham is 100 fils, and, at the time of printing (and since 1980), it was linked to the US dollar at Dhs3.67.

**Money Changers**: More convenient than banks in terms of opening hours and their location in busy shopping areas, money changers also offer better rates than banks. Among them are Al Ansari Exchange (tel: 04 397 7787), Al Fardan Exchange (tel: 04 228 0004), and Thomas Cook Al

**Maps**
Dubai is changing so rapidly that maps of the city quickly become out of date. The best (regularly updated and available at shops across the city) is the *Dubai Map*, published by Explorer Publishing, who also produce a handy, pocket-sized *Dubai Mini Map*.

## Population

Dubai's population is constantly on the rise; around 1.4 million people live in the city, with men outnumbering women by 3:1. Around 90 percent of the total population are expatriates. Asian immigrants account for the bulk of these, and you may well hear as much Hindi, Urdu, Malayalam and Tagalog as Arabic, or possibly even more.

Rostamani (tel: 04 227 3690). All currencies accepted.

**Taxes**: A tax and service charge (usually 20 percent) is added to hotel bills. Check this is included in prices quoted.

**Tipping**: This is not compulsory, and prices in many upmarket hotels and restaurants include a 10 percent service charge. Supermarket employees who pack and carry bags, and petrol pump attendants who clean windscreens, are tipped, but in coins rather than notes.

**Travellers' Cheques**: Easily exchanged at hotels, banks and money changers, travellers' cheques are also sometimes accepted in major shops. Banks are generally open Sat–Thur 8am–1pm only. Money exchanges located in malls and souks keep shop hours.

## P

### PHOTOGRAPHY

Never take photographs of government buildings or military installations. Do not photograph people (especially women) without asking permission.

### POLICE

Dubai's police force has a low-key, but visible presence across the emirate: its green-and-white BMW and Mercedes patrol cars are a common sight on main highways and in residential neighbourhoods. During rush hour, the traffic flow at busy intersections is typically managed by police motorcyclists.

The emergency number for the police is 999. The toll-free number for general information, including details about the force's new Department for Tourist Security, is 800 4438. The police website is www.dubaipolice.gov.ae. *(See also Crime and Safety, p.95.)*

### POST

Dubai's Central Post Office (Sat–Thur 8am–8pm, Fri 5–9pm) is located on Zabeel Road in Karama. There are smaller post offices around the city, including in Deira (near the Avari Hotel), Satwa (near Ravi's restaurant), Jumeira (on Al Wasl Road), in Bur Dubai on Al Fahidi Street opposite the entrance to Bastakiya, and at the international airport.

Sending an airmail letter to Western countries costs around Dhs3–6 and a postcard around Dhs1–2. Allow 10 days for delivery. International courier companies operating in Dubai include DHL (tel: 800 4004), FedEx (tel: 800 4050) and UPS (tel: 800 4774).

## R

### RELIGION

*Islam*

Islam is the official religion of the UAE. Nationals are mostly Sunni Muslims.

*Christianity*

There is freedom of worship for Christians in church compounds on the understanding that they do not proselytise. Christian churches are grouped along Oud Metha Road in Bur Dubai and in Jebel Ali Village. They include Dubai Evangelical Church Centre (DECC, tel: 04 884 6630), the Anglican Holy Trinity (tel: 04 337 0247) and the Roman Catholic St Mary's (tel: 04 337 0087). The main services are held on Friday – the local weekend. Bibles for personal use can be carried into the country.

## S

## SMOKING

In general, the attitude to smoking is similar to that in Western nations. Smoking is banned in all indoor public venues, including restaurants, malls and offices, although you can still smoke in bars and pubs, in most outdoor eating venues, and in most hotel rooms (although a few hotels are now entirely smoke-free). During Ramadan, smoking in public anywhere is forbidden during daylight hours.

## T

## TELEPHONES

Direct international telephone dialling is available from all phones. Local calls within Dubai are free from a subscriber's phone. You should not have a problem finding coin- and card-operated public telephones on the streets and in shopping malls. Pre-paid phone cards are available from Etisalat, shops, supermarkets and service stations. Hotels tend to charge a premium for calls. Roaming mobile users will gain access to the local GSM service. As elsewhere, the code for dialling internationally from the UAE is 00 followed by the relevant national code and local number.

Local telecoms provider Etisalat can be contacted by dialling 101 or 144. The number for directory enquiries is 181. Assistance is provided in English and Arabic. Automated answering systems in Dubai tend to begin in Arabic, so hold on for instructions in English.

The international dialling code for the UAE is 971. Dubai's city code is 04 (omit the zero when dialling from overseas). The prefix for mobile numbers in the UAE is 050 or 055 (again, omit the zero when dialling from overseas). US access codes are as follows: AT&T 800121; MCI Worldcom 800111; Sprint 800131.

## TIME DIFFERENCES

GMT (UCT) +4 hours, BST +3 hours.

## TOILETS

The majority of places have Western-style toilets, although you may occasionally find squat toilets.

## TOURIST INFORMATION

The local Dubai Department of Tourism and Commerce Marketing (DTCM; tel: 04 223 0000; www.dubaitourism.ae) is the emirate's official tourism promotion organisation. DTCM's information centres in Dubai include kiosks in Terminals 1 and 3 at Dubai International Airport, and desks in the following malls: Deira City Centre, BurJuman Centre, Wafi City, Mercato and Ibn Battuta. The head office is on floors 10–12 of the National Bank of Dubai building on the Deira Creekside.

*International Offices:*

**UK:**
4th Floor, 41–46 Nuffield House, Piccadilly, London W1 0DS; tel: 020 7321 6110; e-mail: dtcm_uk@dubaitourism.ae.

**North America**:
25 West 45th Street, Suite #405, New York, NY 10036; tel: +1 212 575 2262; e-mail: dtcm_usa@dubaitourism.ae.

**Australia & New Zealand**: Level 6, 75 Miller Street, North Sydney, NSW 2060; tel: +61 2 9956 6620; e-mail: dtcm_aus@dubaitourism.ae.

**South Africa**:
PO Box 698, 1 Orchard Lane, Rivonia 2128, Johannesburg; tel: +27 11 785 4600; e-mail: dtcm_sa@dubaitourism.ae.

## TOURS

The leading local tour company is Arabian Adventures, a subsidiary of Emirates airline (tel: 04 303 4888; www.arabian-adventures.com), offering an extensive range of tours. Other reliable operators include Alpha Tours (tel: 04 294 9888, www.alphatoursdubai.com), Net Tours (tel: 04 602 8888, www.nettoursdubai.com) and Orient Tours (tel: 04 282 8238; www.orienttours.ae). All of these companies can arrange desert safaris, *dhow* cruises and trips to other emirates.

For hot-air ballooning over the desert contact Balloon Adventures Dubai (tel: 04 285 4949; www.ballooning.ae).

The Sheikh Mohammed Centre for Cultural Understanding (tel: 04 353 6666, www.cultures.ae; *see pp.56*) organises tours of Jumeira Mosque, walking tours of Bastakiya and cultural lunches.

## TRANSPORT

*Airports and Arrival*

The main gateway is Dubai International Airport (tel: 04 224 5555; www.dubaiairport.com), served by the many major airlines including British Airways, Virgin Atlantic, Lufthansa, KLM, Air France, Delta, Air India, Singapore Airlines, Malaysia and Thai. Direct flights from the US are provided by Emirates. The flight time to Dubai

Above from far left: *dhow* in the harbour; Dubai metro light railway.

from Europe is around seven hours; 13 hours from New York.

The airport itself is 10 minutes away from central Deira and a 30- to 45-minute drive from the hotels on the Jumeira coast. The airport comprises three terminals. The sparkling new terminal 3 is where all Emirates flights arrive/depart; terminal 1 is where most other international flights arrive; while terminal 2 is used by smaller regional carriers. Both terminals 1 and 3 have their own dedicated Metro station, as well as tourist information and car rental desks, ATMs and places to exchange money. Regular airport buses also serve the airport, and there are several taxis, although note that taxis picked up at the airport incur a Dhs20 surcharge. The fare from the airport to Deira and Bur Dubai will be around Dhs30–40; considerably more (upwards of Dhs80) to the more distant resorts along the Jumeira coast.

There is no airport departure tax on leaving Dubai.

## Transport Within Dubai

**Nol tickets:** Almost all public transport in Dubai – metro, buses and waterbuses (but not *abras*) is covered by the Nol integrated ticket system (www.nol.ae). You'll need to get a pre-paid Nol card before you can travel. Cards can be bought (or topped up) at any Metro station, at numerous bus stops, or at branches of Carrefour, Spinneys, Waitrose and Emirates NBD Bank. There are four types of card/ticket. The Red Card has been designed for visitors, costing just Dhs2, although this has to be topped up with the correct fare before each journey and can only be recharged ten times; you might prefer the more flexible Silver Card (Dhs20, including Dhs14 credit), which stores up to Dhs500 of credit and lasts five years.

**Dubai Metro**: Since opening in 2009, Dubai's state-of-the-art Metro system (www.rta.ae) has made getting to either end of the city cheaper than before (taxis were often the only option). The system comprises a mix of overground and underground lines, with bright modern stations, although the popularity of the system means that it is often surprisingly difficult to get a seat. The only line currently open is the Red Line, which runs from Rashidiya via the airport and old city and then down through Karama and along Sheikh Zayed Road all the way to Jebel Ali, at the far southern edge of the city.

A second line, the Green Line, is under construction. This will provide a useful loop around the old city centre through Deira and Bur Dubai; it is currently slated to open in the second half of 2011. Trains run approximately every 10 minutes from 6am–11pm Sat–Thur (2pm–midnight on Fridays). Fares start at around Dhs2 up to Dhs7 in standard class, or from around Dhs4 to Dhs14 in the superior Gold Class, which offers slightly plusher carriages.

**Know Your Route** A word of warning: taxi drivers often don't know Dubai as well as you might expect, so, if you can, direct them.

**Taxis**: You'll need to catch a cab to places not covered by the Metro. Cabs are metered, air-conditioned, clean and reliable. The flag-fare is Dhs10 (or Dhs25 from the airport). The main operators are Dubai Taxi, Cars Taxi, Metro Taxi and National Taxi. You can book a cab by calling 04 208 0808, but, they are usually hailed from the street.

**Bus**: Dubai has an efficient modern bus service (tel: 800 9090, www.rta.ae); the main stations are the Gold Souk Bus Station in Deira and Al Ghubaiba in Bur Dubai (from where most services to other emirates depart). Unfortunately, local buses are aimed at low-income expats, and tend not to serve more upmarket tourist destinations. One exception is the handy bus #8, which runs from Al Ghubaiba all the way down the Jumeira Road to the Marina. For longer journeys, however, buses often offer a convenient means of transport – particularly for the traffic-plagued journey to Sharjah, as well as to Hatta, Al Ain and Abu Dhabi.

**Abra**: The best way to appreciate the Creek is to take a water taxi, or *abra (see p.28)*. Fares are just Dhs1 for abra trips from Bur Dubai to Deira and vice versa. For Dhs100 you can charter your own for an hour.

**Water Bus**: Air-conditioned water buses also serve various points on the Creek, costing Dhs4 per return journey (no single fares available), payable only with a Nol card. They're much less enjoyable than the city's *abras*, and are double the price.

**Car**: For a city that didn't have a single stretch of tarmac when oil was discovered, Dubai has excellent roads. All the major car rental agencies have offices here including Avis (tel: 04 295 7121), Budget (tel: 04 295 6667), Hertz (tel: 04 282 4422) and Thrifty (tel: 04 224 5404). Most driving licences will be sufficient; if in doubt, contact your agency in advance.

Remember to drive on the right, always carry your licence with you and never drink and drive – Dubai has a zero-tolerance policy on drink driving and the penalty for ignoring it is a potential jail term. Wearing seatbelts is compulsory for drivers and front-seat passengers, and children under 10 must not sit in the front passenger seat.

Speed limits are normally between 60kph (37mph) and 120kph (74mph). Lane discipline is bad, and reckless driving fairly common, so drive with caution at all times. On road signs, distances are indicated in kilometres.

If you're involved in a road accident, stop and wait for the police. A police report on every level of accident is required for insurance claims.

## VISAS AND PASSPORTS

Visas are available on arrival at

Dubai International Airport for business and leisure travellers from 33 countries, including the UK, Ireland, the US, Canada, Australia, and New Zealand. The visa (free to UK citizens) is valid for 60 days and can be renewed for a further 30 days at the Department of Immigration and Naturalisation (tel: 04 398 1010), near Trade Centre Roundabout, for Dhs500.

Those who don't qualify for a visa on arrival, including South African citizens, can get a 30-day, non-renewable tourist visa through a hotel or tour operator sponsor. This should be arranged before entry to the UAE: visitors should ensure they have a copy of the visa with them and they should stop to collect the original at a designated desk in the airport before they head for passport control. The total cost is Dhs120.

# W

## WEBSITES

The following websites are useful sources of information:
- **7Days** www.7days.ae
- **AMEInfo** www.ameinfo.com
- **Dubai Duty Free**
www.dubaidutyfree.com
- **Dubai International Airport**
www.dubaiairport.com
- **Dubai Municipality**
www.dm.gov.ae
- **Dubai Roads and Transport Authority (RTA)** www.rta.ae
- **Emirates** www.emirates.com

- **Emirates Today**
www.emiratestodayonline.com
- **Government of Dubai Department of Tourism and Commerce Marketing**
www.dubaitourism.ae
- **Gulf News** www.gulfnews.com
- The National www.thenational.ae
- **UAE Ministry of Information and Culture** www.uaeinteract.com
- **TimeOut Dubai**
www.timeoutdubai.com

## WEIGHTS AND MEASURES

The metric system is used in Dubai.

## WHAT'S ON

For listings of events and happenings in Dubai up to 14 days in advance try www.timeoutdubai.com. For planning further ahead, try www.dubai-online.com/events or www.whatsonwhen.com.

## WOMEN

Dubai is one of the easiest places in the Middle East for lone women to travel around, and many feel comfortable on their own in the evening. In terms of personal security, women are generally safe, although it's wise to exercise standard precautions and do not accept lifts from men met in bars and nightclubs. Away from beaches and swimming pools, women are expected to dress modestly, as are men.

**Above from far left:** couple admiring the view; receptionist at a desert resort.

## Bur Dubai

### Arabian Courtyard

Al Fahidi St, Bur Dubai, tel: 04 351 9111, www.arabiancourtyard.com; $$.

Overlooking the Dubai Museum, this attractive four-star hotel could hardly be more central or better positioned for forays into the old city centre. Inside the hotel, there are attractive rooms decorated with Arabian touches and some good eating and drinking options, including the convivial Sherlock Holmes pub.

### Four Points Sheraton Bur Dubai

Khalid Bin Al Waleed Street; tel: 04 397 7444; www.fourpoints.com/burdubai; $$

Right in the heart of the old city, this comfortable and competitively priced four-star hotel makes an excellent base for exploring Bur Dubai and Deira and boasts good facilities including the lovely Antique Bazaar restaurant *(see p.32)* and the cosy Viceroy Pub.

---

The price indicator after each listing is based on two people sharing a standard double room for one night in high season (Nov–April) with tax and service charges included.

| | |
|---|---|
| $$$$ | More than US$1,000 |
| $$$ | US$500–1,000 |
| $$ | US$250–500 |
| $ | Less than US$250 |

---

### Golden Sands

Off Al Mankhool Street, Bur Dubai; tel: 04 355 5553; www.goldensandsdubai.com; $$

A vast number of pleasant self-catering studios and apartments scattered over 11 separate buildings in the Al Mankhool area of Bur Dubai – often some of the cheapest lodgings in town, if you don't mind forgoing some hotel facilities.

### XVA Gallery

Bastakiya; tel: 04 353 5383; www.xvahotel.com; $

No other paid accommodation in Dubai can compete with the XVA Gallery's authentic Arabian offering. More a guesthouse than a hotel – too small to qualify for a star-rating – the XVA is first and foremost an art gallery and coffee shop set around the inner courtyard of a restored home in the historic Bastakiya district *(see p.30)*. Its eight guest rooms, furnished in the Arabian-style, are on the first-floor rooftop, which offers wonderful views of the Creek skyline, in particular the wind towers on nearby buildings.

## Deira

### Hilton Dubai Creek

Deira; tel: 04 227 1111; www.hilton.co.uk/dubaicreek; $$

A pared down, but stylish hotel, designed by architect Carlos Ott with soothingly chic rooms and vast quantities of chrome in the foyer. Its main selling points are Gordon Ramsay's Verre restaurant *(see p.115)* and a rooftop pool with stunning views.

## Hyatt Regency Dubai

Corniche Street, Deira;
tel: 04 209 1234; www.dubai.
regency.hyatt.com; $$

An imposing monolith dominating the mouth of Dubai Creek, the Hyatt Regency has excellent restaurants, including Focaccia *(see p.114)*, and one of the few ice rinks in Dubai. The closest high-quality hotel to Dubai's Gold Souk.

## Radisson SAS Deira Dubai Creek

Baniyas Road, Deira; tel: 04 222 7171; www.deiracreek.
dubai.radissonsas.com; $$

Formerly the InterContinental, this is the oldest five-star in Dubai and still one of the more appealing options in the old city. The hotel has plush décor, a superb selection of in-house restaurants and a brilliantly central location.

### Garhoud

## Park Hyatt

Dubai Creek Golf & Yacht Club; tel: 04 602 1234;
www. dubai.park.hyatt.com; $$$

Rivalling the nearby Raffles for the title of this end of town's top place to stay, this idyllic city retreat occupies a sprawl of Moroccan-style buildings spread along the Creek between the Dubai Creek and Golf clubs, with gorgeous Arabian styling and superb views.

### Oud Metha

## Grand Hyatt

Oud Metha; tel: 04 317 1234;
www.dubai.grand.hyatt.com; $$$

The 674-room Grand Hyatt dominates the highway on the Bur Dubai side of Garhoud Bridge near Wafi City. The hotel is centrally located between the airport, Deira and Sheikh Zayed Road, has several quality restaurants, rooms with stunning city views and an excellent spread of places to eat.

## Raffles

Sheikh Rashid Rd, Wafi, tel: 04 324 8888, www.raffles.com; $$$.

Spectacular hotel *(see also p.46)*, housed in a giant pyramid, with a mix of quirky Egyptian theming and cool Asian designs. There are also superb facilities including huge gardens, a gorgeous spa and excellent restaurants and bars.

### Sheikh Zayed Road and Downtown Dubai

## Armani Hotel

Burj Khalifa, Downtown Dubai;
tel: 04 888 3888,
http://dubai.armanihotels.com; $$$$.

Occupying the lower floors of the Burj Khalifa, the world's first Armani hotel offers pretty much the last word in designer minimalism – although prices are less stratospheric than expected.

## Dusit Thani

Sheikh Zayed Road,
tel: 04 343 3333; www.dusit.com; $$$

A striking landmark on Dubai's main road designed to represent two hands pressed together in the traditional Thai wai greeting. Inside, the Dusit has

**Above from far left:** pool at the Burj Al Arab; a relaxing corner at the Jumeirah Beach Hotel.

**Finding a Deal**
Dubai's hotels are not cheap, and the best deals are likely to be found through tour operators in your country of origin during the northern hemisphere summer. If you call hotels direct, most quoted room rates will not include 20 per cent tax and service charge or breakfast.

**Dubai Districts**
The majority of less
expensive hotels
can be found in
Bur Dubai and
Deira, while the
most desirable
upmarket proper-
ties (with a few
notable exceptions)
are on Sheikh
Zayed Road and
along the coast.
Stretching from
Jumeira through
Umm Suqeim to Al
Sufouh and Al
Mina Al Siyahi, the
coast is commonly
referred to as
'Jumeira'. It may
seem some dis-
tance on maps,
but the hotels in
this area are actu-
ally only 30
minutes' drive from
the airport.

plenty of understated style and the
pretty Benjarong, one of the best Thai
restaurants in this part of the city.

### Fairmont Dubai

Sheikh Zayed Road; tel: 04 332
5555; www.fairmont.com; $$$

Located at the northern end of
Sheikh Zayed Road, the Fairmont is
one of the most luxurious hotels
along the road, with plush rooms, a
decadent spa and a pair of fourth-
floor pools. The space-age interior
also features the popular Spectrum
On One restaurant and Exchange
Grills restaurants *(see p.117).*

### Ibis World Trade Centre

Sheikh Zayed Road/ Trade Centre 2;
tel: 04 332 4444;
www.ibishotel.com; $

This simple, but comfortable, four-
star hotel is perhaps the best value
hotel in the city, although if you want
to get a room, book early, rooms can
get booked up quickly if there's a big
event on at the Dubai International
Exhibition Centre next door.

> The price indicator after each
> listing is based on two
> people sharing a standard
> double room for one night in
> high season (Nov–April) with
> tax and service charges
> included.
>
> $$$$      More than US$1,000
> $$$      US$500–1,000
> $$      US$250–500
> $      Less than US$250

### Jumeirah Emirates Towers Hotel

Sheikh Zayed Road; tel: 04 330
0000; www.jumeirah.com; $$$

Located in the smaller of the two
landmark Emirates Towers, and reg-
ularly voted the top business hotel
in the Middle East. Rooms here
come with stylish, understated décor
and wonderful views, while there are
also superb restaurants and bars
nearby, including Vu's and Al
Nafoorah *(see p.117).*

### The Palace

Emaar Boulevard, The Old Town
Island, Downtown Dubai, tel: 04 428
7888, www.theaddress.com; $$$$

The centrepiece of the atmospheric
Old Town development, this sump-
tuous hotel boasts opulent traditional
Arabian styling and awesome views
of the adjacent Burj Khalifa and
Dubai Fountain.

### Shangri-La

Sheikh Zayed Road; tel: 04 343
8888; www.shangri-la.com; $$$

A striking hotel on Sheikh Zayed
Road, set in a towering, Gotham-
esque structure at the southern end of
the strip. Inside, the hotel is a model
of Zen cool, with beautiful rooms
(many of them offering outstanding
views) and a string of excellent
restaurants.

### Towers Rotana

PO Box 30430, Sheikh Zayed Road;
tel: 04 343 8000;
www.rotana.com; $$

A comfortable business hotel towards the southern end of Sheikh Zayed Road. Fewer frills than other hotels along the road, although with correspondingly lower rates, as well as the bonus of Long's Bar and the pleasant Teatro restaurant, two of the nicer places to spend an evening in the area.

## Jumeira

### Burj Al Arab

Umm Suqeim; tel: 04 301 7777; www.burj-al-arab.com; $$$$

Set on its own island beside the Jumeirah Beach Hotel, the iconic, sail-shaped Burj Al Arab offers the ultimate in luxury. One night in a 225 sq m (2,422 sq ft) 'Panoramic' suite complete with butler service costs around US$1,500. Each duplex has a laptop computer, 114cm (45in) television, Italian marble, Irish linen and ceiling mirrors in the bedrooms. Guests are ferried around in a fleet of white Rolls-Royces.

### Dubai Marine Beach Resort & Spa

Jumeira Road, Jumeira, tel: 04 346 1111; www.dxbmarine.com; $$$

At the northern end of Jumeira, Dubai Marine is the closest beach resort to the city, with attractive rooms in low-rise villas in a landscaped compound fronting on to a small beach. It also has some of the city's best nightspots, including Sho Cho's and Boudoir.

### Jumeirah Beach Hotel

Umm Suqeim; tel: 04 348 0000; www.jumeirahbeachhotel.com; $$$

Designed to look like a wave to complement neighbouring Burj Al Arab's

Left: Jumeirah Emirates Towers Hotel.

If you choose to book into a landlocked hotel in the city, ask if it has a sister hotel on the coast with beachside facilities that you are entitled to use. Among those that do are Le Meridien Dubai, which is situated conveniently close to the airport, and the Jumeirah Emirates Towers on Sheikh Zayed Road.

'sail', the 26-storey Jumeirah Beach has 600 sea-facing rooms, a breathtaking atrium and a plethora of restaurants and bars.

### Mina A'Salam

Madinat Jumeirah, Umm Suqeim; tel: 04 366 8888; www.madinatjumeirah.com; $$$

The less expensive (slightly) of two grand Arabian-themed hotels located within the fabulous Madinat Jumeirah Resort near Burj Al Arab (the other being Al Qasr). Mina A'Salam ('Port of Peace') is an Arabian Nights fantasy linked to Souk Madinat Jumeirah by canals and paths.

## Dubai Marina and Palm Jumeirah

### Atlantis The Palm

Palm Jumeirah tel: 04 426 2000, www.atlantisthepalm.com; $$$$

A vast mega-resort *(also see p.63)* at the far end of Palm Jumeirah – easily the most ostentatious place to stay, although not as stylish as other top-end places in the city. The range of

> The price indicator after each listing is based on two people sharing a standard double room for one night in high season (Nov–April) with tax and service charges included.
>
> | | |
> |---|---|
> | $$$$ | More than US$1,000 |
> | $$$ | US$500–1,000 |
> | $$ | US$250–500 |
> | $ | Less than US$250 |

facilities, including a waterpark, dolphinarium, huge beach and dozens of restaurants and bars, at least partly compensate.

### Grosvenor House

Dubai Marina, tel: 04 399 8888; www.grosvenorhouse-dubai.com; $$$

One of the most alluring hotels in the Marina – not actually on the beach, although guests can share the use of beach facilities with nearby Le Royal Meridien Beach Resort. The style is slick urban cool, while amenities include the ultra-chic Bar 44 (with fantastic views) and a selection of excellent restaurants.

### One&Only Royal Mirage

Dubai Marina; tel: 04 399 9999; www.oneandonlyroyalmirage.com; $$$

One of Dubai's most romantic places to stay, this gorgeous, Moroccan-styled resort sprawls along the beach for the best part of a kilometre. The grounds feature fabulous decor, thousands of palm trees, superb restaurants and the fashionable Kasbar nighclub.

### The Ritz-Carlton Dubai

Dubai Marina, tel: 04 399 4000; www.ritzcarlton.com; $$$

A little bit of Andalusia in the Gulf, the low-lying, hacienda-style Ritz-Carlton has 138 rooms, all of which are sea-facing. More than any other hotel on the coast, it's a quiet retreat for rest and relaxation, far removed from the distractions and crowds of larger beach resorts. Its selection of

restaurants includes the highly rated La Baie (French).

include camel riding, falconry displays and desert safaris.

## Further Out

### Al Maha Resort

Dubai–Al Ain Road (E66); tel: 04 832 9900; www.al-maha.com; $$$$

Meaning 'gazelle' in Arabic, Al Maha offers the most Arabian accommodation in Dubai without any compromise on luxury. Not so much a hotel as a Bedu desert encampment of 30 luxury chalet 'tents' within the Dubai Desert Conservation Reserve *(see p.69)*, this is Dubai's first eco-tourism resort. Activities

### Bab Al Shams Desert Resort & Spa

Endurance City; tel: 04 809 6100; www.meydanhotels.com; $$$

Located in the desert near Endurance City some 37km (23 miles) from Arabian Ranches, the Bab Al Shams ('Gate of the Sun') is popular with city residents as a weekend getaway and it is a good – and significantly cheaper – alternative to Al Maha Resort.

**Camping**
The UAE doesn't have any official campsites, but that doesn't stop local and expat residents camping in the desert dunes on weekends and national holidays. But the best and safest way for visitors to overnight in the desert is with a specialist tour company. Camping on Dubai's public beaches is not allowed without a permit from Dubai Municipality (tel: 04 221 5555).

Left: XVA Gallery.

### Bur Dubai

## Automatic

Al Khaleej Centre, Al Mankhool Rd, also on Jumeira Road, and Sheikh Zayed Road; tel: 04 227 7824; daily 9am–1am; $$

Branch of city-wide budget Lebanese restaurants offering good mezze and grills at very affordable prices. No alcohol. Dress: casual.

## Bastakiah Nights

Bastakiya, Bur Dubai; tel: 04 353 7772; daily 12.30–11.30pm; $$$

Located in an historic courtyard house in Bastakiya, this is one of the city's most atmospheric and romantic restaurants. The menu features a mix of Arabian and Iranian dishes. No alcohol. Dress: smart casual.

## Saravanaa Bhavan

Kahlifa Bin Saeed Building, about 100m east of the Bur Dubai Abra Station, between the HSBC and Bank of Baroda buildings; tel: 04 353 9988, www.saravanabhavan.com; Sat–Thur 7am–3pm & 5.30–11pm, Fri 7am–11.30am & 1.30–11.30pm; $

Of the innumerable bargain curry houses in Bur Dubai, this Dubai offshoot of the popular restaurant chain from Chennai is one of the best, attracting a loyal local following for its delicious, bargain-priced pure-veg Indian cuisine. No alcohol. Dress: casual.

### Deira

## Al Dawaar

Hyatt Regency Hotel, Deira; tel: 04 209 1234; www.dubai.regency.hyatt.com; daily 12.30–3.30pm and 6.30pm–midnight; $$$–$$$$

On the 25th floor of the Hyatt Regency, Dubai's only revolving restaurant boasts stunning views of Deira complemented by an upmarket (if rather expensive) international buffet. Alcohol. Dress: smart casual.

## Ashiana

Sheraton Dubai Creek, Baniyas Rd; tel: 04 207 1733; Sun–Thur noon–3pm & 7.30–11.30pm; Fri & Sat 7.30–11.30pm; $$$–$$$$

One of Dubai's oldest but most consistent upmarket Indian restaurants, specialising in hearty North Indian cuisine served up in rich and flavoursome sauces. A singer and band perform nightly. Alcohol. Dress: smart casual.

## Focaccia

Hyatt Regency, Deira Corniche; tel: 04 209 1234; daily 7pm–midnight, also Fri brunch 12:30pm to 4pm; $$$–$$$$

Upmarket, but pleasantly casual, Italian restaurant with Gulf views and

---

Price guide for a two-course meal for two, with a glass of wine each where alcohol is available:

| | |
|---|---|
| $$$$$ | over Dhs500 |
| $$$$ | Dhs400–500 |
| $$$ | Dhs200–400 |
| $$ | Dhs100–200 |
| $ | below Dhs100 |

a good range of traditional and modern Italian cuisine, with a seasonally changing menu. Alcohol. Dress: smart casual.

### Shabestan

Radisson Blu, Baniyas Rd; tel: 04 222 7171; daily 12.30–3pm and 7–11pm; $$$–$$$$

Arguably the best Iranian restaurant in the city, specialising in huge *chelo* kebabs, fish stews and other Persian specialities, served up to the accompaniment of the resident three-piece Iranian band playing a violin, drum and santour (nightly except Saturday). Alcohol. Dress: smart casual.

### Verre

Hilton Creek, Deira; tel: 04 212 7551, www.hilton.co.uk/dubaicreek; daily 7–11pm; $$$$$

Dubai outpost of UK celebrity chef Gordon Ramsay, and regularly voted one of the top restaurants in the city, Verre is highly recommended if you want to splash out on the chef's superb French-inspired, modern European culinary creations. Alcohol. Dress: smart.

## Garhoud

### Blue Elephant

Al Bustan Rotana Hotel, Garhoud; tel: 04 282 0000; www.blueelephant.com; Mon–Sat noon–3pm and 7–midnight; $$$

A candidate for best Thai restaurant in Dubai located in a quaint Thai-style village. Alcohol. Dress: smart casual.

### Café Chic

Le Meridien Dubai, Garhoud; tel: 04 217 0000; daily 12.30– 2.45pm and 7.30–11.45pm, closed Fri lunch; $$$$$

One of the best French restaurants in the city, this elegant establishment wins regular plaudits for its top-notch Gallic cuisine. The desserts, including hot chocolate soufflé, are particularly good. Alcohol. Dress: smart casual.

**Above from far left:** dish at Al Nafoorah *(see p.117)*; Almaz by Momo *(see p.118)*

**Left:** fine dining at the Madinat Jumeirah.

**Children**
If you are travelling with children, there are activity centres near the food courts at Deira City Centre, Mercato Mall and Mall of the Emirates. Many hotels offer all-you-can-eat brunch specials on Fridays.

## More

Behind Lifco Supermarket, near Welcare Hospital, Garhoud, tel: 04 283 0224, www.morecafe.biz; daily 8am–10pm; $$

A funky Dutch-owned bistro with a wide range of superior international café fare. A difficult place to beat for its combination of excellent atmosphere, quality, value and service. No alcohol. Dress: casual.

## The Thai Kitchen

Park Hyatt, Garhoud; tel: 04 317 2222, www.dubai.park.hyatt.com; daily 7pm–midnight, also Friday brunch 12.30–4pm; $$$$

One of the best and most romantic Thai restaurants in town, set on the Park Hyatt's idyllic Creek-side terrace and offering a sumptuous range of unusual regional specialities. Alcohol. Dress: smart casual.

### Oud Metha
## Asha's

Wafi; tel: 04 324 4100, www.ashasrestaurants.com; daily 12.30–3pm and 7.30–midnight; $$$–$$$$.

Owned by legendary Bollywood chanteuse Asha Bhosle, this Wafi restaurant offers a good range of Indian classics alongside more unusual regional specialities, including recipes from Asha's own cookbook.

## Khazana

Al Nasr Leisureland, Oud Metha; tel: 04 336 0061; www.sanjeevkapoorskhazanadubai.com; daily 12.30–2.30pm and 7–11.30pm; $$$

Owned by Indian celebrity chef Sanjeev Kapoor, Khazana does excellent North Indian specialities in a village-style conservatory setting. Alcohol. Dress: smart casual.

## Medzo

Wafi, tel: 04 324 4100; 12.30–3pm and 7.30–11.30pm; $$$

A suave little restaurant offering top-notch Mediterranean cuisine in a stylish but laidback setting. Mains are around Dhs80.

### Karama
## Chhappan Bhog

Sheikh Khalifa Bin Zayed/Trade Centre Road, Bur Dubai; tel: 04 396 8176; daily 12.30–2.30pm and 8–11.30pm; $–$$

The North Indian vegetarian meals served here are so delicious that they will please the taste buds of even the most die-hard meat eaters. No alcohol. Dress: casual.

### Sheikh Zayed Road
## Après

Mall of the Emirates; tel: 04 341 2575; daily 10am–midnight; $$$

Chic bar and restaurant overlooking the slopes of Ski Dubai and offering a good range of international fare – anything from coq au vin to fish and chips – backed up by one of the city's best cocktail lists. Dress: smart casual.

## The Exchange Grill

Fairmont Hotel, Sheikh Zayed Road;

tel: 04 311 8559,
www.fairmont.com/dubai; Sun–Thur
12.30–3.30pm and 7pm–midnight,
Fri and Sat 7pm–midnight; $$$$$
The city's most exclusive steakhouse,
this small and very upmarket establishment serves up choice gold
Angus and Wagyu cuts, backed up
by one of the city's most extensive
wine lists. Dress: smart casual.

## Al Nafoorah

Emirates Towers, Sheikh Zayed
Road; tel: 04 319 8088;
www.boulevarddubai.com; daily
12.30–3pm and 8pm–12.30am; $$$
One of the top Lebanese restaurant's
in town, with a great-value lunch
menu and pleasant terrace. Look out
for Sheikh Mohammed, who is pur-
ported to drop in from time to time.
Alcohol. Dress: smart casual.

## Spectrum On One

The Fairmont Dubai, Sheikh Zayed
Road; tel: 04 311 8101;
www.fairmont.com/dubai; daily
7pm–1am; $$$$
Suave multi-cuisine restaurant serving
up a vast selection of top-notch inter-
national fare – including Indian,

Chinese, Japanese, Arabian and
European – from its six different show
kitchens. Alcohol. Dress: smart casual.

## Trader Vic's

Crowne Plaza, Sheikh Zayed Road,
and Souk Madinat Jumeirah; tel: 04
331 1111; www.tradervics.com;
daily noon–3pm and 7pm–2.30am;
$$$$
A happy mishmash of styles –
Polynesia meets Asia and the
Caribbean – this upbeat bar and
restaurant has live music and a
party atmosphere. Alcohol. Dress:
smart casual.

## Vu's

Emirates Towers Hotel, Sheikh
Zayed Road; tel: 04 319 8088;
www.jumeirah.com; daily
12.30–3pm and
7.30–midnight; $$$$$
Inventive fusion fine-dining, with a
mix of European and Asian influ-
ence, plus stunning views from the
50th floor of the landmark
Emirates Towers hotel. Vu's bar,
downstairs, is a fine place for a pre-
or post-prandial drink. Alcohol.
Dress: smart.

## Jumeira

## Al Mahara

Burj Al Arab, Umm Suqeim;
tel: 04 301 7600; www.burj-al-
arab.com; daily 12.30–3pm and
7pm–midnight; $$$$$
Centred on an enormous fish tank,
this spectacularly designed subter-
ranean seafood restaurant is one of

**Above from far
left:** alfresco dining
at Beachcombers;
Gordon Ramsay's
stylish Verre.

**Friday brunch**
The Dubai Friday
brunch is a city
institution,
equivalent to the
British Sunday
roast. It's
particularly popular
amongst the city's
European expat set,
while many
restaurants lay on
all-you-can-eat (and
sometimes drink, as
well) deals. Brunch
usually kicks off
around midday, and
can last for the
remainder of the
afternoon.

> Price guide for a two-course
> meal for two, with a glass
> of wine each where alcohol
> is available:
>
> | $$$$$ | over Dhs500 |
> | $$$$ | Dhs400–500 |
> | $$$ | Dhs200–400 |
> | $$ | Dhs100–200 |
> | $ | below Dhs100 |

Dubai's most expensive, with sumptuous international seafood. Alcohol. Dress: smart.

## Almaz by Momo

Harvey Nichols, Mall of the Emirates, Sheikh Zayed Road; tel: 04 409 8877; Sat–Thur 10am–midnight, Fri 10am–1.30am; $$$

Dubai version of the celebrity hangout in London, offering mezze and traditional Moroccan mains in a trendy, contemporary North African-themed interior. No alcohol. Dress: smart casual.

## Al Qasr

Dubai Marine Beach Resort & Spa, Jumeira Road; tel: 04 346 1111; www.dxbmarine.com; daily 12.30–3.30pm and 7pm–2am; $$$$

An upmarket Lebanese restaurant with a wide-ranging menu of mezze and grills, plus shisha and live music with belly dancing later in the evening. Alcohol. Dress: smart casual.

## Beachcombers

Jumeirah Beach Hotel, Jumeira; tel: 04 406 8999; www.jumeirahbeachhotel.com/dining; daily 12.30–4pm and 6.30–11.30pm; $$$

This Southeast Asian restaurant with a thatched terrace overlooking the spectacular Burj Al Arab is difficult to beat for its views. There's an à-la-carte menu for lunch and buffet for dinner. Families are welcome. Alcohol. Dress: smart casual.

## Pai Tai

Al Qasr Hotel, Madinat Jumeirah; tel: 04 366 6730;

**Right:** Pierchic.

www.madinatjumeirah.com; daily
6.30–11.30pm; $$$$

This is one of the city's most romantic places to eat, with live music and stunning Burj Al Arab views from the candlelit terrace. The menu features all the usual Thai classics, including spicy salads, and meat and seafood curries. Alcohol. Dress: smart casual.

### Pierchic

Al Qasr Hotel, Madinat Jumeirah; tel: 04 366 6730;
www.madinatjumeirah.com; daily 1–3pm and 7–11.30pm; $$$$$

So romantic and oh so chic, this international seafood restaurant at the end of its own wooden pier offers stunning views of Burj Al Arab and the Madinat Jumeirah resort. Alcohol. Dress: smart.

### Sho Cho

Dubai Marine Beach Resort, Jumeira; tel: 04 346 1111;
www.dxbmarine.com; daily 7pm–2.30am; $$$

This fashionable hang out for Dubai's beautiful people overlooks a small beach and is part sushi restaurant and part cocktail bar and nightclub. Alcohol. Dress: smart casual.

### Zheng He's

Mina A'Salam, Madinat Jumeirah; tel: 04 366 6730;
www.madinatjumeirah.com; daily noon–3pm and 7–11.30pm; $$$$

One of the top Chinese restaurants in Dubai, with sumptuous décor and superb classic and contemporary fare. Alcohol. Dress: smart casual.

## Dubai Marina

### Indego

Grosvenor House Hotel, tel: 04 399 8888, www.grosvenorhouse-dubai.com; Sun–Thur 7pm–midnight; $$$$

Overseen by Vineet Bhatia, India's first Michelin-starred chef, this stylish restaurant showcases Bhatia's outstanding contemporary Indian cooking, with a seductive blend of sub-continental and international ingredients and techniques. Alcohol. Dress: smart casual.

### Rhodes Mezzanine

Grosvenor House Hotel, tel: 04 399 8888, www.grosvenorhouse-dubai.com; Mon–Sat 7–11.30pm; $$$$$

Dubai outpost of UK celebrity chef Gary Rhodes, with a short but inventive menu showcasing Rhodes' distinctive brand of modern European cuisine, accompanied by classic British puddings like jam roly-poly and bread and butter pudding. Alcohol. Dress: smart casual.

**Above from far left:** Vu's and its sky-high views; Zheng He's.

**Snacking**
For a traditional snack between meals try a *manouchet zaatar*, Arabic bread with thyme, sesame seeds and olive oil, or *manouchet jebneh*, Arabic bread with cheese. These are best eaten straight from the oven at one of the numerous Lebanese bakeries in the city.

Price guide for a two-course meal for two, with a glass of wine each where alcohol is available:

| | |
|---|---|
| $$$$$ | over Dhs500 |
| $$$$ | Dhs400–500 |
| $$$ | Dhs200–400 |
| $$ | Dhs100–200 |
| $ | below Dhs100 |

Nightlife in Dubai is a mix of the traditional and the contemporary. For many local Emiratis, after-dark activity consists largely of sitting back over endless cups of coffee, shooting the breeze and watching the world go by while puffing away on a shisha (waterpipe) – a lot easier on the nose than your average smoke-fogged pub. Elements *(see p.45)* in Wafi, Kan Zaman in Bur Dubai *(see p.32)*, and Shakespeare & Co. on Sheikh Zayed Road *(see p.52)* are three good places. Many parts of the old city also come alive at night, particularly in Deira, when the neon comes on and the souks fill up with shoppers, ranging from local expat Indians and Pakistanis through to European tourists, Russian bargain-hunters and West African gold traders.

In terms of more contemporary entertainment, the city boasts a superb selection of bars and a reasonable club scene, kept going by a flow of eager tourists, Western expats and the city's smart Lebanese party set. Cultural attractions are relatively thin on the ground, unless your visit coincides with a major event like Art Dubai, or the jazz and film festivals *(see p.74, 97 and 98)*.

## Bars

### 360°

Jumeirah Beach Hotel; tel: 04 406 8769; www.jumeirah.com; nightly from 7pm–late; closed June–Aug; occasional entrance charges

Principally a bar, although also hosts local and visiting DJs. Whatever's on offer, this is one of the city's finest chill-out spaces, overlooking the coast, JBH and Burj Al Arab from the end of a long breakwater – a great place to crash out over a beer or shisha.

### Bahri Bar

Mina A'Salam Hotel, Madinat Jumeirah; tel: 04 366 6730, www.jumeirah.com; daily 4pm–2/3am

One of the most captivating bars in Dubai, with beautiful Moorish décor, artefacts and to-die-for views over the Madinat Jumeirah to the towering Burj Al Arab opposite.

### Neos

63rd floor, The Address, Downtown Dubai; tel: 04 436 8888; www.theaddress.com; daily 7pm–2am

One of the highest bars in Dubai, with jaw-dropping views across to the Burj Khalifa and Downtown Dubai and a chic interior – although the spangly metallic décor isn't to everyone's taste.

### RED Lounge

Raffles, Wafi; tel: 04 324 8888; www.raffles.com; Tue–Sat 6pm–2/3am

Occupying part of the spectacular glass-walled pyramid at the top of the Raffles hotel, with superb views and very cool, Chinese-themed décor, backed up with top-notch dim sum and a wide range of cocktails.

## Sho Cho

Dubai Marine Beach Resort; tel: 04 346 1111; www.dxbmarine.com; daily 7.30pm–2am or later

The sea-facing terrace bar at this small Japanese restaurant remains one of the prime places to pose in town, attracting a mix of tourists and beautiful people from the local Lebanese party set. The resident DJ (Sun and Wed–Fri) provides a suitably mellow chill-out soundtrack.

## Skyview Bar

Burj Al Arab; tel: 04 301 7600; www.jumeirah.com; daily noon–2am

Landmark bar almost at the top of the Burj Al Arab, with psychedelic décor and vast sea and city views. The drinks menu is particularly strong on cocktails (from Dhs100), but you'll need to reserve in advance and there's a minimum spend of Dhs225 per person.

## Vu's Bar

Jumeirah Emirates Towers Hotel; tel: 04 319 8088; www.jumeirah.com; daily 6pm–3am

One of the loftiest licensed venues in Dubai, on the 51st floor of the Emirates Towers hotel building, with futuristic décor and huge views out through the wall to ceiling windows. Also boasts one of the city's biggest drinks lists.

## Clubs

## Boudoir

Dubai Marine Beach Resort; tel: 04 345 5995; www.myboudoir.com; nightly 9pm–3am

This over-the-top bar-cum-nightclub attracts some the city's most showy residents, who come to strut about the club's decadent interior (looking like a kind of plush, 19th-century Parisian brothel) whilst consuming indecent quantities of champagne.

**Above:** Bar 360.

**Club Nights**
Clubs in Dubai come, go and change name and DJ on a regular basis. Check out the latest listings in *Time Out Dubai* or visit www.platinum list.ae to find out where's new and hot.

**Left:** Bahri Bar.

Music includes a mix of hip hop and house, with occasional visiting international DJs.

## Chi@The Lodge
Al Nasr Leisureland, Oud Metha; tel: 04 337 9471; www.chinightclub dubai.com

The biggest club in the Middle East, with room for 3,500 revellers in its four different areas, each with its own soundtrack, and an eclectic music selection. The club's big main outdoor dancefloor is particularly popular. Hosts regular big-name international DJs and occasional bands. Entrance charges vary depending on who's playing, and you can expect to queue later at night, particularly at the weekend.

## Kasbar
The Palace, One&Only Royal Mirage, Dubai Marina; tel: 04 399 3999; Mon–Sat 9.30pm–3am

Catering to an older and relatively sedate crowd (over 25s only), this upmarket club shares the opulent Moroccan styling of the rest of the Royal Mirage complex. Music is usually a mix of Arabian and international tunes. It get's lively at times, but if things are slow it's worth checking out the nearby Rooftop Bar, which also has live music most evenings.

## Zinc
Crowne Plaza Hotel, Sheikh Zayed Road; tel: 04 331 1111; www.myspace.com/zincdubai; nightly 10pm–3am

One of the longest running clubs in Dubai, known for its relaxed atmosphere, eclectic soundtrack and general reputation for unpretentious partying. Music features a mix of retro, R&B, hip hop and house depending on the night.

## Live Music
### Dubai Media City Amphitheatre
Increasing numbers of well-known international rock and pop acts are visiting Dubai. Concerts are usually held at the Dubai Media City Amphitheatre, with a capacity of 15,000 (it also hosts the annual Dubai Jazz Festival, *see p.97*). Check *Time Out Dubai* (www.timeoutdubai.com) for upcoming gigs.

### El Malecon
Dubai Marine Beach Resort; tel: 04 346 1111; www.dxbmarine.com; nightly 6.30pm–late

A colourful Cuban bar, restaurant and club rolled into one, with walls covered in graffiti and live Latin bands during the night; 9am–11am (except Sat, when there are salsa classes), followed by a DJ.

### Jambase
Souk Madinat Jumeirah; tel: 04 366 6730; www.jumeirah.com; Mon–Sat 7pm–12.30am (drinks until 2am, or 2.30am on Thur–Fri)

This place serves as a bar and restaurant early in the evening, turning into a fun, unpretentious live music venue later at night, hosting a variety of

enthusiastic local cover bands, often with a Latino slant.

## Peanut Butter Jam

Wafi, Oud Metha; tel: 04 324 4100; www.wafi.com; Fri from Oct–May 8pm–midnight

Laidback music evenings held on the open-air rooftop terrace of the Wafi complex. Sink into a giant beanbag under the stars and listen to local jazz musicians and pop bands performing a mix of cover versions and assorted original tunes.

### Performing Arts

## Dubai Community and Arts Centre (DUCTAC)

Mall of the Emirates, Sheikh Zayed Road; tel: 04 341 4777; www.ductac.org

One of the few places in the city keeping the cultural flicker alight, DUCTAC is home to a trio of lively little venues: the Centrepoint Theatre, Kilachand Studio Theatre

and Manu Chhabria Arts Centre, which host a wide range of productions, including film, music and theatre (several shows aimed at children), with the emphasis on local and community-based projects.

## Madinat Theatre

Madinat Jumeirah; tel: 04 366 6546; www.madinattheatre.com

Dubai's first proper theatre when it opened in the mid-noughties, although don't expect much beyond a fairly predictable range of mainstream musicals, children's shows and other crowd-pleasers.

## The Palladium Dubai

Media City; tel: 04 363 6897; www.thepalladiumdubai.com

A fairly new state-of-the-art entertainment venue that hosts a very mixed range of events including regular stand-up comedy nights and live music shows through to international seminars and awards ceremonies.

**Above:** Skyview Bar.

**Ladies Only**
Ladies Nights are a Dubai institution. These are usually held on Wednesday, Thursday or, most commonly, Tuesday nights in an attempt to drum up custom during the quieter midweek evenings, with lots of places around the city offering all sorts of deals for girls, ranging from a couple of free cocktails up to complimentary champagne all night. Pick up a copy of *Time Out Dubai* (or check www.timeoutdubai.com) for listings.

**Left:** Jambase.

# CREDITS

**Insight Step by Step Dubai**
**Written by**: Matt Jones
**Updated by:** Gavin Thomas
**Commissioned by:** Tom Le Bas
**Edited by:** Pamela Afram
**Series Editor**: Sarah Sweeney
**Map Production**: APA Cartography Department
**Picture Manager**: Steve Lawrence
**Art Editor**: Ian Spick
**Production**: Tynan Dean and Linton Donaldson

**Photography by**: Apa: Matt Jones except:
APA/Kevin Cummins, 73T, 74TL, 75TR, 76T, 77T, 80-81, 81Abu Dhabi Tourism, 88M, 88MT, 88TR, 89TL, 89TR,90TL, 90TR, 91TL; Atlantis the Palm, 64MB, 64MC, 64MT, 64T, 65T; AWL Images, 8-9, 19T, 48TL, 54TL, 55TR, 60-61, 62TL, 63TR, 82T, 83T, 87; Corbis 11B, 11TR, 23T; Dubai Aquarium and Underwater Zoo, 52MB, 52MC, 52MT, 52T; Dubai Mall, 50TL, 51TR; Dubai Tourist Board 11TL, 12TL, 14TL; Ferrari World, 7BR; Fotolibra, 48-49; Fotolia, 2-3; Getty 16TL, 34T, 36T, 65B, 94–5; istockphoto 2BL, 2BM, 2BR, 2ML, 2MM, 2MR, 10TR, 12B, 12TR, 13TL, 16TR, 24-25, 24ML, 35T, 46-47, 53, 54B, 62-63, 74-75, 85T, 96, 97; Jambase, 123; Jumeirah, 48B, 58-59, 58TL, 59B, 110T, 114T,115B,120-121, 121B, 122-123; Photolibrary, 37B, 37T, 44-45, 45T, Pictures Colour Library, 54-55; Raffles Hotel, 47B, Superstock, 43T, TopFoto, 22T; Wafi Mall 44TL,

**Front cover**: main image: Corbis; bottom left: superstock; bottom right: istockphoto.

**Printed by**: CTPS-China

©2011 Apa Publications (UK) Limited
*All rights reserved*
Second Edition 2011

No part of this book may be reproduced, stored in a retrieval system or transmitted in any form or by any means (electronic, mechanical, photocopying, recording or otherwise), without prior written permission of APA Publications. Brief text quotations with use of photographs are exempted for book review purposes only. Information has been obtained from sources believed to be reliable, but its accuracy and completeness, and the opinions based thereon, are not guaranteed.

Although Insight Guides and the authors of this book have taken all reasonable care in preparing it, we make no warranty about the accuracy or completeness of its content, and, to the maximum extent permitted, disclaim all liability arising from its use.

## CONTACTING THE EDITORS

We would appreciate it if readers would alert us to errors or outdated information by writing to us at insight@apaguide.co.uk or APA Publications, PO Box 7910, London SE1 1WE, UK.

**www.insightguides.com**

# DISTRIBUTION

*Worldwide*
**APA Publications GmbH & Co. Verlag KG**
**(Singapore branch)**
7030 Ang Mo Kio Ave 5
08-65 Northstar @ AMK, Singapore 569880
Email: apasin@singnet.com.sg

*UK and Ireland*
**Dorling Kindersley Ltd**
**(a Penguin Company)**
80 Strand, London, WC2R 0RL, UK
Email: sales@uk.dk.com

*US*
**Ingram Publisher Services**
One Ingram Blvd, PO Box 3006
La Vergne, TN 37086-1986
Email: customer.service@ingrampublisher
services.com

*Australia*
**Universal Publishers**
PO Box 307
St. Leonards  NSW  1590
Email: sales@universalpublishers.com.au

# INDEX

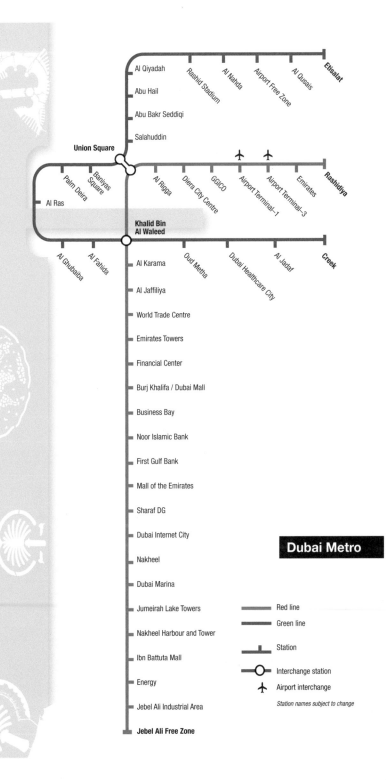

Al Qiyadah
Abu Hail
Abu Bakr Seddiqi
Salahuddin

Union Square

Rashid Stadium
Al Nahda
Airport Free Zone
Al Qusais
Etisalat

Palm Deira
Baniyas Square
Al Ras

Al Rigga
Deira City Centre
GGICO
Airport Terminal–1
Airport Terminal–3
Emirates
Rashidiya

Khalid Bin
Al Waleed

Al Ghubaiba
Al Fahida
Creek

Al Karama
Oud Metha
Dubai Healthcare City
Al Jadaf

Al Jaffiliya

World Trade Centre

Emirates Towers

Financial Center

Burj Khalifa / Dubai Mall

Business Bay

Noor Islamic Bank

First Gulf Bank

Mall of the Emirates

Sharaf DG

Dubai Internet City

Nakheel

Dubai Marina

Jumeirah Lake Towers

Nakheel Harbour and Tower

Ibn Battuta Mall

Energy

Jebel Ali Industrial Area

**Jebel Ali Free Zone**

## Dubai Metro

Red line

Green line

Station

Interchange station

Airport interchange

*Station names subject to change*

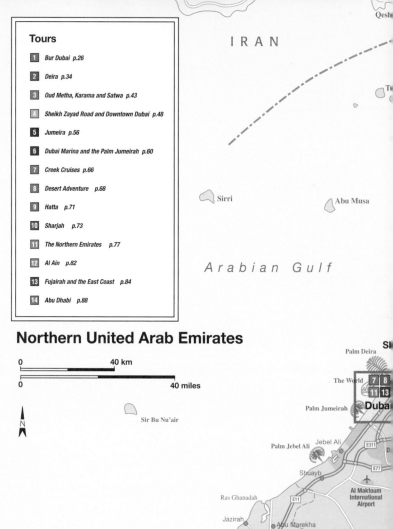

## Tours

# Northern United Arab Emirates

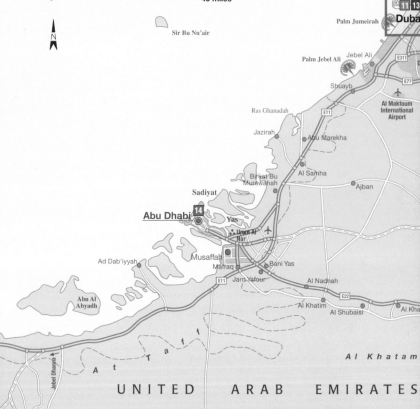

IRAN

Qesh

Te

Sirri

Abu Musa

*Arabian Gulf*

0       40 km

0       40 miles

N

Sir Bu Nu'air

Palm Deira

Sh

The World   7   8

11   13

Palm Jumeirah   Dubai

Palm Jebel Ali   Jebel Ali

Jebel Ali   E311

D

E77

Shuayb

Al Maktoum
International
Airport

Ras Ghanadah   E11

Jazirah

Abu Marekha

Birkat Bu
Murawāhah   Al Samha

Sadiyat    Ajban

Abu Dhabi   14   Yas

Umm Al
Nar

Ad Dab'iyyah

Musaffah

Mafraq   Bani Yas

Jebel Dhanna

Abu Al
Abyadh

E11   Jaru Yafour

Al Nadhah

Al Khatim   E22   Al Khaz

Al Shubaisi

*At   T a f f*

*Al Khatam*

UNITED     A R A B     E M I R A T E S